FRONT

CW00972352

A SOLDIER'S STORY

STEVE STONE

Copy editing by Chantelle Cross-Jones
ISBN-13: 978-1517263867
ISBN-10: 1517263867

FOREWARD

Frontline offers an insight into the life of just one soldier out of the many thousands in the British Infantry deployed to Afghanistan. These modern day heroes risk their lives on a daily basis to help bring peace to a troubled country.

Some of these soldiers are fresh out of school, or college, and within a few months find themselves in a war zone fighting for their lives. The book gives a candid account of life on the front line. The highs and the lows of fighting a war thousands of miles from home, whilst at the same time battling homesickness, and coming to terms with death and injury on a daily basis. Imagine being 18 and sent to a foreign country with 40-degree heat, an environment that is dusty and areas that are quite inhospitable. Every step on a dusty track could be your last as your eyes strain to catch a glimpse of an IED, before it is too late. That is before you get to where the enemy actually are, and the rounds start impacting in the dirt all around you, kicking up small puffs of dust.

Islamic Republic of Afghanistan is the official name for Afghanistan. It has no coastline, as it is a landlocked country, located in the centre of Asia. Afghanistan has a population of about 29 million, and covers an area of 250,001 square miles. Afghanistan is bordered by China in the far northeast, Turkmenistan, Uzbekistan and Tajikistan in the north, Iran in the west and Pakistan in the southeast. The land in the country has been fought over for thousands of years, even the British Army suffered a bitter defeat in 1842.

The War in Afghanistan, also known as the Afghan war, began on October 7th 2001. It started when the Northern Alliance formed from the armed forces of the United Kingdom, United States of America, Australia, and the Afghan United Front. Together they launched Operation Enduring Freedom. The attacks on September 11th, 2001 were the real precursor, they showed the need to remove the al-Qaeda terrorist organization and end its use of Afghanistan as a base. Locating Osama Bin Laden, who was reported to be in Afghanistan, was another reason for the war in Afghanistan.

The United States wanted to remove the Taliban regime from power so they could support in the creation of a viable democratic government. With over a decade into the war, the Allied Alliance continues against the Taliban insurgency that has become more widespread, and the war has even expanded into the tribal areas of neighbouring Pakistan. It has been a long and hard fought war, which many would suggest has not actually improved or helped Afghanistan. Afghanistan is a war of politics as much as a war between soldiers, where diplomatic solutions and getting Afghanistan to be politically stable are as important as getting rid of the Taliban.

All the troops out in Afghanistan are true heroes fighting a war thousands of miles from home, in hostile conditions with danger and death being faced on a daily basis. They do come back as changed men and women after seeing the true horror of war first hand.

PROLOGUE

Three months into my tour and some days, it was like a living hell. Our platoon had just been tasked to recce an area for a new Forward Operating Base (FOB). The rationale for looking at a new FOB was to try and protect the far side of our area, whilst at the same time protect the main road running through it, which served as an egress route used by the Taliban after placing Improvised Explosive Devices (IEDs) and ambushing conveys. Command wanted an FOB there because of the high enemy activity. We had the Marines for support if needed, but they were pretty tied up dealing with insurgents in their locality and were having much more contact than us.

We had some attachments including a mortar group and could call in air support if needed. Two lads and I along with a LSW (Light Support Weapon) which is an SA80 with a slightly longer barrel and a bi-pod made up the bulk of the firepower, along with a (GPMG) General Purpose Machine Gun. We finally made it to the new suggested FOB site. The area was quite flat with nothing but patches of long grass and sun baked earth. Trees surround two sides of the field, which would offer us some protection if we were attacked, even if it did block our field of view and meant the flip flops could use the trees to sneak up on us.

Most of us went into all-round defence; whilst a couple of the lads did a Barma which is army speak for searching an area for IEDs. After well over an hour, the site was found to be clear, so we got ourselves dug in for the night. With our entrenching tools, we dug in the hard sun baked soil, which turned to dust the moment you dug into it. The temperature was now in the 40s, but after three months of the heat, you grew acclimatised to it - even if for the first few weeks, you were drinking virtually non-stop. The heat now felt no worse than a hot sunny day in Britain.

We had a quiet night with no contact, but none of us were allowed to sleep as the chances of being attacked were extremely high. As the dawn began to break, a large burst of 7.62mm PKM fire snapped over our heads and landed in the hard sun-baked soil with a shallow thud.

The PKM is a modernised Russian GPMG and lethal in the right hands. I was in a world of my own, and it took a few seconds for my mind to realise what was going on. The GPMG opened up, as did the whole platoon. We focused on the direction the fire came from, as our eyes searched for muzzle flashes to be better able to get a fix on the Flip Flop position. Then, all of a sudden, the enemy fire seemed to get heavier. More rounds were landing amongst us - almost as if it had started raining heavily.

I remember seeing tracers whizzing past my head and hearing the gunfire that seemed to cut out all other sounds. As I let out another burst after changing magazines, I heard a very large screeching sound followed by two thuds behind us. I looked around and saw two clouds of dust and smoke from where the RPGs had landed, and my section commander yelling "RPGS, FUCKING RPGS!" We continued to lay down rounds and then heard a very large shout for the medic, meaning we had a casualty.

The enemy fire seemed to have moved to almost encircle us by now. I looked back to assess the situation and the dark Afghanistan twilight was lit up by red and green tracers. It was almost surreal. It made me think I was in a movie or a video game as opposed to real life. The Flip Flops had set up in a tree line a couple hundred meters out. They had used a PKM, a modernised version of the PK both of which are a single bipod light machine gun of Russian origin. They had used this to distract us whilst the main force got into position behind us.

Another RPG came crashing down on us and this time I felt the blast push me back, followed by a subsequent shower of dirt that landed on me. My mate lying next to me was bleeding from the neck. A piece of shrapnel from the RPG had lodged in his neck. It wasn't too bad, but at this point in time it was too dangerous to try patching him up. With the intense firefight now going on behind us, we were ordered to move and lay down fire to the front. By now, our mortar team had opened up, and was laying down effective fire on the enemy. Now we were all returning fire from our dugouts as rounds were raining down on us. A rocket had whizzed by no more than a foot from my head. The scream deafened me and I couldn't hear my own voice.

As we set up in our new position, the entire tree line looked like it was flashing; it was like a large firework display, only this firework display was deadly. It was impossible to count all the muzzle flashes, but there seemed an awful lot of them. Pyrotechnics and rockets lit up the dawn sky, almost like there was a constant sun. Mortars continued to rain down into the tree line, and this finally allowed us to gain the upper hand. I saw two Flip Flops running along the ridgeline just to the left of us; I let out a burst and saw one drop. The other Flip Flop was also dropped a few metres later. I could barely stick my head out of the hole I was in, with rounds impacting all around us, kicking up small clouds of dust.

Finally, we heard a jet overhead, a Harrier GR9 offered fire support in the form of two 540lb bombs, which were dropped on the Flip Flop position. The noise and the force of the blast from these two bombs were immense. The shock waves rattled our position. The muzzle flashes ceased and all the echoes and dust clouds from the planes took over the scene. I had experienced the awesome power and destruction of air support before, but it still left me in awe. Thank God for it too, otherwise I don't think we would have survived. Thank God, the fighter jocks are good at hitting the right spot, as it was getting dangerously close!

A signal to cease fire was given by the platoon commander, and sent down the chain of command until the entire platoon was yelling the command. At this point, it all went eerily quiet, and the ringing in my ears began. By now, my mate had his whole neck wrapped in gauze. Trying to remove the shrapnel in the field might cause it to bleed more, so pressure was applied around it. He was not the only casualty; we had lost another man due to enemy fire. A bullet had somehow managed to penetrate his head just above his right eye, but below the front of his helmet. It was one of those once in a million chance shots from a stray bullet, my fellow soldier just happened to be in the wrong place at the wrong time.

This was the second of the lads to be killed by a bullet in a week. Only last week Private Brown had climbed up the ladder to the rooftop position on the fort, to begin his stag behind the GPMG. He was briefed by Corporal Harris to stay low after seeing two suspicious characters moving 200 metres to the front. He could not make out any weapons, but there could well be Flip Flops. Today had been a day when we had received more direct fire than usual from various locations. After an hour, a couple of the lads shouted up at Brown to tell him what they would be having for tea. Brown lifted his head up slightly to reply when they heard the sound of a high velocity round.

The lads below saw his helmet fly off, and shouted, "Man down! Man down!" I span around to see Brown's shoulders slump forward, and ran over. One of the lads climbed the ladder and saw blood gushing onto the sandbags from the back of Brown's head. As the Sergeant ran up the ladder, Brown was slumped down with his mouth and eyes wide open. He was clearly unconscious and had a single bullet wound to his forehead. We dragged him down and removed his body armour while we waited for a medevac. Another corporal got on the GMPG and let off some rounds from where he thought the bullet had come from. This was done more out of anger and frustration than hope of hitting anything. The Flip Flops responsible, after having seen Brown go down, knew there would be a reprisal and would have been quick to get away. Brown died on the helicopter on the way to Camp Bastion, and was confirmed dead when he arrived. I got the pleasant job of removing the blood soaked sandbags and replacing them.

As the dust and smoke settled in the FOB, the air was filled with the smell of cordite and a hint of burnt flesh.

Several Flip Flop's lay dead to our front, and there were probably more in the trees. The Flip Flops would recover their dead once we had gone, which would be soon as we packed up quickly and prepared to leave. I took a deep breath and said thank you for surviving yet another fire fight, the worst so far. Happiness filled me and I let out a huge sigh of relief.

As my adrenaline rush calmed down, and paranoia settled in, I looked around and noticed some of us were filled with euphoria whilst others looked terrified. All of us thought about what had gone wrong and why we had ended up in an ambush. The main question was: how did so many of them get so close? As was so often the case, intelligence that expected light resistance had been wrong again; we had just encountered heavy resistance.

The Flip Flops would sometimes use up to 30 fighters to launch simultaneous attacks against us and a local checkpoint manned by the local police. It had been overrun several times prior to our arrival. There was little doubt that the Flip Flops still held sway in our area of operation. In the last month, alone two police officers had defected to the Flip Flops as they offered better pay and living conditions. With them, they took two PKM machine guns, which were later to be used against us. The Flip Flops used coercion and brutality to enforce their authority, but just like us, they were trying to win the locals over. The on-going lack of manpower in the area still meant the Flip Flops pretty much had free reign, although we were told we were making steady progress and inroads. Without air power, I am sure we would have become surrounded or even overrun at our beloved fort.

One day Captain Green took a 13-man patrol, along with six Afghan police, to check out a new area of activity that was seeing the locals being harassed.

An hour into the patrol, a local warned the Afghan police with us that the Flip Flops were in a number of the compounds nearby. The patrol split up, with half moving to one compound and the other half moving to another compound. A hand-launched Desert Hawk surveillance drone was launched and immediately observed four possible Flip Flops moving into another compound. Minutes later the Flip Flops attacked from the compound roof using machine guns and an RPG. The patrol was split and pinned down. The intercepted walkie-talkie messages indicated that the enemy was very close to the patrol's position, and were preparing to reinforce their numbers with more fighters. An air strike was called in, and it wasn't long before two Royal Air Force

Harriers were on station. The fire was becoming more intense and a Quick Reaction Force, made up of the rest of us at the fort, was sent out. The patrol by now was in a full fighting retreat as we made our way out. The Harriers were ordered to stand down for fear of hitting civilians as they only carried 500lbs bombs. An Apache helicopter had been dispatched but was at least 15 minutes away. The patrol didn't have 15 minutes as they were running low on ammo, and luck.

As we approached a bridge over the canal, which was always a vulnerable point, I was at the front doing my occasional Barma. I have to admit it makes you almost scared shitless to move, thinking that every step you take could be your last, or you might miss an IDE and someone else is killed. You almost wish that nothing will be detected by the Vallon, because when it does start beeping you know that you will have to get down on your belt buckle and confirm if an IED is present or not, while all the time thinking, "I would not of joined the army if I knew I would be doing this, I'm no expert and don't really know how to deal with these devices." Every time you see the aftermath of an IED, especially a bad one where a mate is now in a thousand pieces, you always think, "It could be me next."

Behind me was the interpreter, and 3 metres to his left Private Jenkins. Suddenly there was a massive explosion followed by a ringing in my ears. I turned round to see Jenkins in a bad way - killed instantly - and the interpreter had taken the full force of the blast and ended up decapitated. I had holes in my trousers and combat jacket. The horror and thought that I was to blame, even though it was a low metal content IED, which my Vallon would not have been able to detect, has never left me to this day. After that, my nerves were in tatters and I was never able or even asked to Barma again. I still have nightmares and wake up to the smell of human flesh in my nose.

Whilst we were busy clearing up the bits of body and bagging them up in various body bags, the patrol we were meant to support made it back, more by luck than anything else. The Flip Flops had heard the Apache approaching due to the distinctive noise from its rotors, and retreated, giving the patrol a chance to make good their escape. The fleeing Flip Flops were picked up by the Apache - a well-placed Hellfire took over half of them out, with the rest succumbing to a few rounds of the Apaches 30mm cannon.

CHAPTER ONE

In 2010, almost at the end of my six-month tour, I was laying out in the heat of Afghanistan being seriously injured. After being placed onto a stretcher, I was carried back with non-life threatening injuries and luckily still conscious, when the stretcher bearer, out of the blue said to me:

"Is this all really worth it?"

For the life of me, I couldn't answer his question. After more than a year in the Army I couldn't, on the spur of the moment, say exactly why I was there and it really was worth it.

The Army had been my life so far, and my only real chance of employment after gaining poor grades at school and then being kicked out of my home and college. I decided to join The Mercian Regiment, a light role infantry battalion.

We infantrymen are the soldiers who are specifically trained for the role of fighting on foot, to engage the enemy face to face and historically have been known to bear the brunt of the casualties of combat in wars. We are the oldest branch of combat arms, or the fighting arm that forms the backbone of the army. All Infantry units have a more physically demanding training regime than other branches of the military, due to being on the frontline spearheading attacks, which calls for a higher level of physical fitness and discipline.

We like to think of ourselves as better soldiers compared to those who are trained to fight in armour or in technical roles, such as armourers or signallers. Basic infantry skills are fundamental to the training of any soldier, and soldiers of any branch of the Army are expected to serve as auxiliary infantry (patrolling and security) when necessary.

I had no real knowledge of life outside of Derby, and Afghanistan was just a place on the news. In all honesty, when Afghan was mentioned, I would usually turn the TV over to something more interesting. The furthest I had been was Scotland and we spent many summer holidays at one coast or another in England.

After thinking about joining up I did start to get excited watching war programs on the TV, such as "Ross Kemp in Afghanistan", and the brochures I got from the recruiting office made being in the Army seem like one great big adventure.

On second thought, I won't say that it was purely love for adventure that made me join. There may have been, in the back of my head, a wish to see the world and a chance to move away from Derby, which I had outgrown and grown bored of. I saw no future for myself in Derby at that time, and I seemed to be forever arguing with my parents about one thing or another.

Whatever my motives for joining the British army, they did not have time to crystallize until I had been wounded and sent to Selly Oak Hospital. While recuperating at Selly Oak I had time to acquire a perspective as to why I had really joined the Army. I knew we had been fighting for the greater good and trying to make the world a safer place, even though at the time I thought the war in Afghanistan was pointless. After seeing friends die and injured I wanted to kill the Taliban in revenge for what they had done to my mates. I'm not sure if that was the right motivation, but it kept me going during the low times of my deployment.

I finally decided to join up in June 2009. My first thought was to go into the Royal Logistic Core or 'Loggies' in Army slang. Everyone said, "Get a trade" but nothing seemed to really appeal.

In the end, I decided on somewhere there would be fighting, I wanted to be on the front line and I wanted "some action." Deciding to go into a fighting arm would mean joining the Mercian's as an infantryman.

On a cold February morning, I left for Derby Station to begin my journey to my new life in the Army. The final part of the journey, after the train, was on the number X27 bus. The bus seemed full of new recruits all high on excitement. Most of them had obviously been drunk the night before, and the bus had the smell of stale larger and sweat.

Perhaps the less said about that the last part of the journey the better. I just sat and read through a leaflet I had on Catterick.

It made out that Catterick Garrison was almost a country club, with bars, restaurants and sports facilities. It read just like a holiday brochure, which made Catterick almost sound a better place to be than a hot sandy beach in Barbados. The last time I read something like this was before I went on holiday to a Butlin's holiday camp. It did seem like a great place to live for a while and undertake my initial training.

All too soon, we had made it to the Infantry Training School at Catterick and the bus pulled up with a screech of its brakes. We all filed off one by one and made our way to the main gate.

CHAPTER TWO

Being late February, Catterick seemed so bleak; the camp was almost in the middle of Catterick. I felt cut off from the outside world the moment I stepped through the front gates into the base. It was a very different world to the one I was used to, with its own rules and regulations.

Catterick was my first time away from home. Living in Army barrack accommodation was not like living at home, and high standards and rules of behaviour were expected. We also had to keep everything spotlessly clean.

The Accommodation was in a 1950s looking large brick building, with different wings for various course groups.

I would share the accommodation with other members of my course; we had eight in our room. All beds were 2ft 6in wide and 6ft long, on a grey steel frame and fitted with a thin green PVC covered mattress. I was allocated a double wardrobe, as well as a footlocker that sat at the end of the bed and was used as extra storage space. We had shared shower, bath and sink facilities, as well as a drying room, for getting wet and muddy kit dried off.

We were shown to our shared quarters, and the first night was quite a noisy one. Most of the lads were snoring, and the lad sleeping next to me was going at it with his mouth wide open, breaking all records. Most of the beds sagged like an old hammock.

I was up early, and directed to the place across the camp where we were to eat. The "Cookhouse" would be where we ate three hearty meals a day, starting with an early breakfast. These meals were supposed to be balanced and healthy, but nearly always ended up with Chips somewhere in the combination. At least there was always my favourite desert, Angel Delight, virtually every day.

The first day was spent doing quite a bit, of what the Corporals called, "Admin." 'Admin' in Army speak meant cleaning and getting your 'shit' sorted. Along with the Admin was a physical examination. After that, I was taken to an office where I had to swear my allegiance to the Queen by placing my hand on a bible. The Officer then told me

I was now a member of the Mercian's. We had a quick chat about what I had done in my life so far, and future aspirations.

During our training, we learnt that being a soldier is about putting others first, and having the courage and knowledge to do the right thing in any given situation. You worked as part of a team, and had to be able to rely 100% on your mates.

One of the best elements of the training was the camaraderie; you made strong bonds with each other. You all experienced the same training regime together, which was both physically and mentally challenging at times. A few lads did drop out though, as they couldn't take the hard regime. Some would cry in their beds at night, especially the young 16 year olds who became homesick. The older lads acted as big brothers to us. One lad had been in the Territorial Army and already knew most of what to do. He was a great help having already served in Afghanistan, and was now training to be a full-time soldier, before he went out to Afghanistan for another 6-month tour.

I found 'Personal Administration' quite a funny term to begin with. It is everything to do with looking after yourself and your kit, in the field as well as in camp. The training was designed to help us become more organised and precise, and help us learn to do things instinctively.

Weapons Training was one of my favourite parts of the course. We learnt how to handle the SA80 rifle, which is the main weapon used by British forces. The SA80 was not particularly well thought of when it came into service in 1985, with persistent issues of stoppages, magazines falling off and plastic parts breaking in extreme climates. We also got to use an LSW, a GPMG and night viewing devices. We started our training on simulators before moving on to ranges and field firing exercises. Finally, there was a five-day live firing exercise at the end of the course.

Drill Training meant military procedures and movements, such as marching and parading. I found drill very difficult and was so bad they decided to have me in the middle rank. On one occasion, I was on the outside when the order for "Right wheel" was given, I marched off to the left all on my own. Drill was to aid in discipline, as well as taking pride in our appearance. A soldier who looks after themselves better will better survive when out in the field.

The fieldcraft element was where we learnt the basic skills we needed to be able work and survive in the field. We looked at how to conceal ourselves and move without being noticed. We also practised map reading and setting up an OP (Observation post). These skills were tested in exercises during the course, with a final large-scale exercise that spanned a couple of days.

I enjoyed the field craft, but I remember one that nearly made me quit. It was April and still bitterly cold, so cold that it had been snowing. We had been issued with winter rations, which were on their use by date; this was fine except being boiled rice and rehydrated food they needed plenty of water and heat to cook. The normal boil in the bag stuff could be eaten hot or cold.

I had been ordered to go out and put out trip flares. These were just a flare with a long wire attached that would go off if walked through, alerting everyone to a potential attack.

This had taken so long that it was getting dark. As soon as I started cooking my food, I was ordered to stop and put out the fire I was using. The food was still raw but I attempted to eat the semi raw rice and peas anyway, along with a cup of tepid tea.

The night temperature really dropped, and even in my sleeping bag, I was shivering like a leaf. I have never been so cold in my life, I almost felt like I was on the verge of hypothermia. However, if I gave up I would be back squaded and have to redo the previous three weeks. I just had to ride the night out, but it felt like the longest night ever. The next day warm sunshine woke me up, although I still felt rather ill as I emerged from my Basha made from bungee cords and a waterproof sheet.

The next night was not much better, we all had to dig trenches and sleep in them. Only these just filled with water and mud. I spent my second night sleeping in muddy water. The sleeping bags had a Gortex outer that they could be put in so at least you stayed semi dry. It felt like I was sleeping on a waterbed. By the time we got back to camp, all of us were covered head to toe in mud. I had the best hot shower ever, before starting the enormous task of getting my kit clean.

There was lots of varied exercise to build up our stamina and strength during the course, including gym work, running, swimming and assault courses. The PTI's (Physical Training Instructors) worked us hard, pushing us harder and harder to the point you would be physically sick.

Adventurous Training was another important part of the course and quite good fun. I have been able to do things I had never done before. I was able to undertake sports and activities I never dreamed I would be able to do. A constant theme of all the training we undertook was the importance of working as a team and looking after your mates.

The first few weeks were a routine of parades, inspections, drill, classroom training and physical education. It was a hard and difficult routine, which for some was just too much. You would often be up until midnight and beyond preparing your kit and room for inspection the next morning.

After a few weeks, when we were hardened somewhat, they began to throw us into night exercises. This meant us going out at ten o'clock in full kit, and yomping several miles. Catterick is a large training area and very hilly in places. In late February, it was very wet and cold as well.

In the first two months, I completed the weapons course on the SA80 and found I was quite a good shot; I was on track to be a true marksman. Besides that, I became mentally as hard as nails and had learned thoroughly the system of discipline.

The next course I was sent on was the 26 week Combat Infantry Course (CIC). It was designed to teach recruits both the basic soldiering skills we needed, along with the main elements of being an infantry soldier. After completion of the CIC, I was posted to my battalion as a newly qualified infantry soldier with still much to learn.

I was sent to Belfast, Northern Ireland. Belfast, I had been told, was a popular posting with officers and soldiers. I was also told there are many advantages to being based in one of the UK's major cities. When off duty, there was a lot to do – we could even travel to the Irish Republic, and were able to explore the whole island. Palace Barracks where we were based was just two minutes from Belfast City Airport and five minutes from the ferry terminal. We were still given an extensive brief on safety though, especially since the Massereene Barracks shooting on the 7th March 2009, when two off-duty soldiers of the 38 Engineer Regiment were shot dead right outside the Barracks. Two other soldiers and the two civilian deliverymen were shot and injured during the attack as well.

The attack happened at around 21:40, when four British soldiers, who were off duty, had walked outside the barracks to pick up a pizza that had been delivered. As they passed the pizzas over, two gunmen in a nearby green Vauxhall Cavalier opened fire with Heckler & Koch G3A3 battle rifles. The firing lasted for more than 30 seconds with more than 60 shots being fired. After the initial shots, which wounded the victims, the gunmen walked over to them and fired again at close range, killing two of the soldiers. A few hours later, the car involved was found abandoned eight miles from the barracks. The soldiers were all wearing desert fatigues and were to be deployed to Afghanistan the next day.

The Mercian's are basically a light role infantry battalion; we're meant to be rapidly deployable and could find ourselves being the first into a battle zone ahead of heavier forces and equipment that required longer preparation times. With basic training complete, I had further choices in what I might want to specialise and train in. For example, there was an Antitank Platoon - equipped with the JAVELIN missile system, and a Communications and Information Systems Platoon - that operate the BOWMAN digital radio system. The BOWMAN consists of a range of HF radio, VHF radio and UHF radio sets that are used to provide secure integrated voice data services to soldiers on foot and vehicles and command HQs, all the way up to Division level.

I decided just to be an infantryman for the time being and could not wait to see some action.

The Mercian's had deployed to Afghanistan in no less than three other occasions in the last five years. They were seen as one of the most experienced units in the British Army in that theatre of operations. I was told, we would return to Afghanistan later on in the year.

After training, I got a week's leave and was invited by one of my mates to spend the leave with him, at his home in Nottingham. I knew very little about Nottingham, other than from the odd visit and the rumour about there being five girls to every boy, or something like that. I suspect it had more to do with Robin Hood and men in tights, and that all the real men had run off! My mate's family took me in as if I was an extra son, and made me feel at home from the minute I came through the front door. They took me into their hearts with a simple hospitality and kindness I would never forget. I did enjoy being in Nottingham, even if Nottingham Forest were the arch rivals of my home team Derby County.

After my few days of leave things moved fast. I was back in Ireland continuing training, and we would soon be starting special work-up training ready for deployment to Afghanistan.

Personally, I could not wait to be deployed, but the veterans seemed much more reserved about it. I never really showed my excitement, just got on with the training and worked hard. I had made up my mind early on that I was a very small pebble on a very large beach, and it was better to obey orders and keep my mouth shut.

The work-up training seemed to last for weeks, and we even had a mock up Afghanistan village with various scenarios set up. The scenarios range from casualty evacuation to raiding a house for an insurgent. I loved the scenarios and it just made me want to get to Afghanistan even sooner. The Gurka's wives would often play the civilians and the Gurka's the actual enemy.

We spent days on the range homing our shooting skills and going through the various skills and drills. Our weapon was the most important bit of kit, being able to unload and know what to do if it stopped working was drilled into us constantly.

The worst part of weapons training was the cleaning afterwards. You ended up with all these bits from your weapon in your cap and each one had to be cleaned.

I got on really well with the rest of my fellow riflemen and seemed to fit in well. I got all the usual sheep shagging jokes, because I came from Derby.

The day of deployment came up really quick, and we were ushered on to coaches to make the trip to the airport before flying "Royal Air Force Airlines" to Afghanistan. The weird bit was the VC10 we flew in had rear facing seats instead of forward facing ones. Apparently, this is to increase survival rates in the event of a crash. The plane landed with a slight thud at Kandahar airport before taxiing to a stop. I looked out of the window and could see the RAF ground crew scurrying around the plane as the engines wound down.

As soon as I got off the plane, the heat hit me along with the dry dusty atmosphere. It was like opening the door to a very hot oven at 42 degree Celsius, which was the most intense heat I have ever felt. The terrain seemed quite barren with only the odd splash of green dotted about, and large mountains in the distance.

On the first night, we were to be billeted at Camp Bastion, before getting a Chinook to take us to our point of operations in the village of Dishu in Helmand Province.

Camp Bastion is the main British base in Afghanistan with over 21,000 personnel being based there. The sergeant was telling me it was the biggest overseas British military camp built since World War II. The camp is situated in a remote desert area quite high up and far from population centres. It is about Four miles long by two miles wide, with an airstrip and a field hospital. The base is divided into 2 main parts, including two tenant camps; Camp Barber (US) and Camp Viking (Danish). Bastion also adjoins Camp Leatherneck (US) and the Afghan National Army (ANA) Camp Shorabak. Apache and Chinook helicopters are also forward-deployed at the Heliport.

The base had everything from a cinema to various takeaways and shops. It was like a small town in itself.

We had several briefings to attend before we could depart; one of them was on IEDs. We were bussed to a corner on the south side of the runway for our IED class. They showed videos, confiscated from insurgents, of them killing soldiers; vehicles that had been blown up, medics being shot. They walked us around a hanger full of disarmed bombs collected from the countryside, and they had constructed mock areas like the ones on village roads to show how IEDs were planted. The idea was to both shock us and make us think about IEDs. They were the single biggest killer of soldiers in Afghanistan.

Next, we went to the sexual assault briefing. The sexual assault brief was regrettable and disturbing in the sense that soldier-on-soldier rapes are common enough to warrant it. Although it was a much bigger issue in the US Army than the British Army. War could do strange things to people, although some had a hidden darker side before they joined up.

The next day we climbed aboard the Chinook to make our way to Dishu. Like other settlements in the district, it is located near the Helmand River. The population was about 9,482. We would be stationed in an old fort pockmarked with gunfire from both the Taliban and the previous Russian occupation.

The British Army term the Helmand area the 'Green Zone', due to the flat patchwork quilt of irrigation canals, ditches and fields that are full of crops, and provide such an ideal defensive battleground that it is easy to set up attacks and lay IEDs. Also due to the grid system of roads in the towns and a lattice of narrow crumbling tracks that restricted military movement, and channelled convoys through choke points. The Flip Flops however enjoy total freedom of movement by being able to wade across canals and use motorbikes over the rickety bridges positioned every hundred yards or so. Flip Flops would even open or close sluice gates to alter water levels or flood areas to impede or channel military movement. Flip Flops are not to be underestimated, they are very skilled tacticians and very adept at creating ambushes or setting up IEDs. The 'Green Zone' is quite a long yet thin area around the Helmand River, towards the mountains it is pure desert that even the Nomads find far too difficult to cross - a tank would become stuck in the fine dusty sand within a few metres.

The Americans built the various irrigation ditches and channels in the 1970's and these same irrigation channels are the one the Taliban have been able to use to their advantage. The narrow tracks alongside the channels are the ideal place to plant and conceal an IED. Many of the tracks caused convoys to be funnelled down set routes, which offered ideal ambush sites. Going cross-country is not an option due to the damage the convoys would cause to legitimate farmland, causing an outcry from the locals. Crossing points are few and far between, less the odd rickety wooden footbridges that are ideal for Taliban on foot or even on a motorbike to ingress or egress to place an IED, or launch an ambush.

Our allocated bed area would be the old cowshed within the fort; it smelt as if a few cows had already died in there.

On the first night, mortar fire came down almost as a welcoming celebration from the local Taliban or Flip Flops in Army slang and sounded pretty close.

Now and again, a mortar would burst nearby with a kind of hollow, "Bang", but for some reason we didn't seem to mind, maybe we knew that if mortars were coming down we were that little bit safer. Thankfully, the Flip Flops only spent an hour trying to shell us and I could get my head down for the rest of the night.

A message came down from Camp Bastion at daybreak that we were needed to go out on patrol and clear any Flip Flops from the surrounding area.

We were lucky, or was that unlucky to have six Afghan National Police assigned to us. Which we thought was great initially; however they were soon stealing food and getting under our feet. They had brought along a catamite, who was a young boy brought as their sexual plaything. A couple of days later our sergeant discovered an Afgan Policeman and a catamite under a blanket and shouted 'stop making love'. All the Policemen had deserted the base by the next day.

Homosexuality and paedophilia in Afghanistan is quite high because of the tradition in which adolescent boys are cherished for their beauty and apprenticed to men to learn a trade. In Islam homosexuality is strictly forbidden - however cultural interpretations of Islamic teachings prevalent in Pashtun areas of southern Afghanistan tactically condone it in comparison to heterosexual relationships. It cites women are for children, boys are for pleasure. For an Afghan man to have sex with a boy was considered a, 'Forbile' whereas intercourse with an 'ineligible woman' could cause issues of revenge and honour killing. For me it was weird and extremely difficult to understand.

The British soldier loves to moan about anything and everything. They never seem happy unless they are unhappy. We all especially hate having things added to our kit, and you cannot blame us, in full equipment we are certainly all dressed up like a pack-horse. The armour we wore added to the weight and discomfort, especially in a very hot climate.

We had the enhanced Mark 7 helmets and Osprey Assault body armour which provided ballistic protection, and was more comfortable than previous body armour.

The armour system is modular and built around a vest, which covers your torso. The protective elements to cover your upper arms and around the neck and throat can be added to the main vest. The vest has webbing tape so we could attach extra pouches or equipment to it.

The vest has a front and rear soft armour panel, which join with the aid of fasteners and press studs on the shoulders and waist. The panels themselves contain a ceramic plate to stop rifle rounds both front and rear, and is in itself protected by a rubber surround to avoid wear and tear. The Mark 7 helmets offer limited protection as a well-placed rifle round could still penetrate. More often than not though our helmets would manage to deflect the bullet and stop a fatality.

I won't say that the body armour is that light or that easy to wear over a long period, but could well save your life. We were all told the story of Lance Sergeant French who was working on the radio at a CP (Command Post) in Babaji when he felt something hit his helmet, and then heard something drop on the floor.

He thought some of the lads on sentry duty were throwing stones at him as a joke, so he started to shout some abuse at them. Then, in an instant, he realised what had happened - a grenade had been thrown and bounced off his helmet. On realising this he shouted,

"GRENADE" and dived on the floor. It was not clear where the grenade had actually landed; but he just dived right on instinct.

Thankfully, French's instinct was correct. He hit the floor, literally only a split second before the grenade detonated. He was less than a metre from where it exploded

After the blast, French just looked like he had fallen into a prickly bush. His only visible wounds were a few scratches on his face caused by flying debris. His ears were ringing for a couple of days after and he suffered some blurred vision. Shrapnel had become embedded in his armour but without his armour he would most probably been killed.

I found one Platoon was a good lively bunch. Lance Corporal Wells was the best of the lot, and we became good friends. He taught me many things, including how to carry out my new duties and tips on how to survive my first deployment. This was his second deployment.

The base was not quite how I expected; my previous idea of a field camp had been a roomy set of tents, maybe a bit dusty, but comparatively comfortable. Our, cow shed hole was about four and a half feet high, you had to get in doubled up on your hands and knees - about seven by ten feet on the sides, and the floor was covered with very dirty straw and cow shit. Everyone else was already smoking on their hammocks, but boy this place stunk to high heaven.

Ten of us with all our equipment were packed in here. We were told that if the Flip Flop attacks were reduced or stopped, then they might look towards better accommodation in the centre of the fort. However, for now the cow shed was one of the safest places. The Officers had a large room next to the operations room with the radios and other communication equipment.

I crowded up into a corner and set up my sleeping area. The lads didn't seem overly glad to be there, and moaned a great deal about the crowding and smell. They regarded me with extra disfavour because I was the new boy, fresh from training with no field or battle experience.

"Oy sheep shagger you can go in the corner" said one soldier.

They were a decent lot of lads though.

"I want to go see me woman and shag her brains out"

"Only women you ever had is the blow up variety" cut in another soldier

Then a fresh-faced lad chirps up, "The last doll he had, became deflated he was that bad!"

That was met with universal groans for being such a bad joke.

So on it went about women and food. Food was pretty much all we thought about even though the scoff at the camp was ok. The Asian cook we had could do some mean curries.

They were in the midst of a discussion about what part of the body was most desirable for a wound to get you home early, when a young officer decided to pay us a visit. He was a second lieutenant, quite fresh out of Sandhurst, and in command of our platoon.

Second Lieutenant Meakin seemed really nice. He shook hands with us newbies and said he hoped we would become valued members of the platoon. Then he told us there was to be a patrol the next night and he was looking for volunteers.

Nobody spoke at first and all looked at each other, but I finally broke the silence and volunteered. I had already broken the first unwritten Army rule – "Never volunteer".

I think I spoke more to break the embarrassing silence than anything else. I think that I was led a little by a kind of youthful curiosity - it may be that I wanted to appear brave in the eyes of these soldiers who so evidently held me more or less in contempt as a newcomer.

Meakin accepted me, and one of the other new men offered. He was taken on for the patrol as well.

After Meakin left, Sergeant Page told us we had better get some sleep while we could. Sleep in this case meant closing our eyes and dozing.

In the morning, I began to itch, and found I had made the acquaintance of the soldier's enemy, the "Mossie". The mosquito loved fresh clean skin, and seemed to love UK skin the most. I had forgotten to apply insect repellent. Big mistake! Sometimes when I get to thinking about it, I believe a mosquito has bitten me and start to scratch.

The other constant problem for many of the lads in Helmand was 'D & V', Diarrhoea and Vomiting, and most weeks at least one of the lads was suffering from it.

CHAPTER THREE

In the morning, all of us due to go out on Meakin's patrol were taken to one of the rooms in the fort, there we were given instructions before carrying out a rehearsal. This was Meakin's first, "Real" patrol, and the CO was anxious to make sure it was a success. Including Meakin, there were ten in the patrol. Meakin then beat our instructions into us until we knew them by heart. Even if his initial explanation was full of stutters, and some of the lads took the piss out of him, he seemed to know what to do.

Meakin had not long been commissioned; he'd just finished his Platoon Commander Battle Course prior to our deployment. He was originally from Melton Mowbray, Leicestershire, but had attended Durham University to do some degree or other. Being unable to find work, he decided to join the Army as an officer.

The object of the patrol was to get into the enemies area by stealth, take out as many as possible, take prisoners if possible for intelligence reasons, and finally get out without any casualties.

We spent the day getting prepared and sorting our kit. Just before dark, we went straight to the cookhouse for a good tea before some kip. The final bit of prep was to apply camouflage cream to our faces. This was always done to prevent the whiteness of our skin from showing under any form of light, and helped us to be more covert under the cover of darkness. Although if you leave the camouflage cream on too long you had more spots than a teenager.

The time set for our patrol was midnight. Then we were to head out of the fort to a known Flip Flop location about a mile and a half away. Intelligence said it was only occupied by two or three lightly armed Flip Flops.

We moved up to the attack position just before one am. At zero minus ten, that is, ten minutes before one, our mortar team opened up. It was the first full on battle I had ever been in, and it seemed as though all the mortars in the world were raining down. Afterwards I found that it had only been a light mortar bombardment on the objective.

Meakin came dashing up, very excited as it would soon be time to move in on our objective. It was a very dark night and I could just make out the silhouette of the compound. I could feel my heart racing and the adrenaline pumping round my body.

The barrage of fire kept up right to zero hours, as per schedule. At 30 seconds to one. I looked at my watch and the din was at its height. At exactly one, it stopped short. The Flip Flops were still firing with their AK-47's but comparatively there was silence after the intense noise from the barrage of mortar fire.

With the silence, we quickly made our way towards the compound, going up and down every 5 feet in a motion called, "pepper potting". The Flip Flops were still firing, but they seem to hit very wide of the mark.

The compound was still 100 feet away. We dropped and started to crawl. I skinned both my knees on a rock or something, along with both my hands. Using my rifle in battle worried me, as I was afraid of jabbing a Flip Flop with the attached bayonet. They were attached, just in case it turned into a close quarter's battle. I had yet to kill anyone, and I was as much fearful having to kill as I was of being killed.

The bayonet is a scary looking weapon that slips in easily but is not quite so easy to remove. It even has the aptly named, "Blood channel" to aid in its removal from your victim.

As I moved towards the objective, I spent those few minutes wondering which bullet had my name on it as the 'Ack, Ack' of AK-47's still rang out.

I had the same, "Gone" feeling in the pit of my stomach that you have when you drop fast in an elevator or on a fairground ride. The skin on my face felt tight, and I remember clenching my teeth. Adrenaline coursed through the veins of my body and I seemed just to be focused on the objective in front of me. I had no idea who was to the left or right of me.

As we got within 50 feet of the compound, a Flip Flop on the roof spotted us and started yelling something in Pashto to the others.

Instantly all manner of hell broke loose, they must have got every available machine gun firing on us, but their aim was way off. One of the corporals got up and ran towards the compound. When he got close enough he threw a grenade through a window. A few seconds later, an enormous bang was followed by a large cloud of dust and smoke.

It seemed to subdue some of the firing or that could have just been wishful thinking on my part. We got up and all started running towards the compound, but I spotted a Flip Flop 20 feet away from my position. For an instant, I stood frozen to the spot, and then it flashed through my mind what I had to do when in such a situation. I tried to remember what I had been taught and get my mind to start working and formulating a plan. I was now most certainly in fight or flight mode.

This hesitation did not last more than a second and I continued moving forward.

Then, out of the corner of my eye, I saw the Flip Flop raise his weapon towards me and I fired. Why that Flip Flop did not fire straight away, I will never know. Maybe he did fire and missed, at the time I was too focused on firing my weapon. I fired several rounds, which actually turned out to be a full magazine of 30 rounds. We were always taught to count the number of rounds we had fired. In the heat of the moment, I just let rip. He dropped to the floor and lay motionless. I stood for a few seconds my hand shaking from the adrenaline still pumping through my body. I had no time to think about what had just happened - I was shouted at to move forward.

We then started to move into the compound. We found a machine gun and threw another grenade. Two or three Flip Flops appeared, and started running towards us, several of the men opened up and they fell to their knees.

We continued to search the compound, but found no one else. One of the rooms was full of weapons and components to make bombs or IEDs. The haul of weapons and bombs seemed more important to some of the lads than killing some Flip Flops. Corporal Barnes had lost a mate to IEDs on their last tour. He was on a mission to locate and get rid of as much IED making paraphernalia as he could. It was his last words to his dying mate as he lay in his arms.

We were looking at out haul when we heard Meakin calling us together. He had gone off with four of the lads to do a final check and make sure the compound was clear. Once clear the idea was to call in air support, they would drop a 500lb bomb and destroy the compound so the Flip Flop's could not reuse it. Why they had not dropped a 500lb bomb in the first place I will never know. Who am I to question tactics, with just a few months service and no experience of war?

With the compound cleared Meakin called in air support and we quickly got out of there. A 500lb bomb could do a lot of damage, and we needed to be a few hundred feet away for safety.

The roar of a jet plane, followed by a slight whistle and an enormous bang as a 500lb bomb impacted on the compound. The compound was completely flattened to nothing more than a pile of rubble.

Meakin got a commendation for the night's work; I got two enormous blisters, cut knees and hands, and a bollocking for not counting my rounds and using 30 rounds on one Flip Flop. I still felt numb, I don't think it had really dawned on me that I had just shot and killed someone. It was not until I got home to the UK that the nightmares started, when I am the one who has been hit and can feel myself falling to the ground.

CHAPTER FOUR

After the good kicking, we had given the Flip Flops on the patrol; they behaved themselves reasonably well for quite a while. It was the first raid that had been undertaken in the area for quite some time. No doubt, it may have caught the Flip Flops off guard. However, they would soon regroup and set up a new base, hopefully slightly further away from Dishu.

For quite a while afterwards the Flip Flops seemed a bit, well, "Windy." They would send up the odd mortar or set up an IED that would be tripped by cattle, just to keep us on our toes.

The next night my section was tasked with going and supporting some Special Forces. A Special Forces unit near to us had captured a significant Flip Flop financier. We arrived at the compound where they had detained him to help out. The sun would be up in an hour and they would be leaving. They had done their jobs well, absolutely no one was hurt and they got all the suspect men away from the family. I remember walking through a blown-open wooden door to see thirty women and children sitting on various blankets. The inside courtyard smelled not too dissimilar to our cow shed back at the fort. Farm tools lay all around the courtyard. I could hear crackles of radio traffic in an unfamiliar language spoken by the armed men inside their home. They all looked visibly terrified. The Special Forces told my section commander what they had undertaken here, and within ten minutes, helicopters whisked them away.

After the sun rose and the warmth enveloped the courtyard, I got a better picture of what had occurred. All the men had been tied up, wearing blindfolds and were shirtless. They had been numbered with permanent markers on their forehead. This was to make it easier to take note of what had been seized from what individual and saved time trying to write complex names.

The owner of the property told us that we had got the right person. A business associate; had asked him for shelter. The Pashtun hospitality code meant he had to offer his business associate shelter. We took the owner around the property to make sure he noted any damage or theft caused by the raid. Other than clothes, which were strewn on the floor where the Special Forces had just dumped them, they had for once not managed to cause any damage. The children's bedroom had two-dozen backpacks hanging on the wall: Afghans usually have big families. After the tour of his property, the owner said there had been no damage and understood it had been a lawful search.

The rest of the women and children were of no concern so our Afghan National Police counterparts herded them back indoors to a room we had already searched, and we left them to it. With everyone in the property sorted and as happy as they could be. The Afghan National Police took all the suspected Flip Flops away for questioning and we could go back to our fort.

It turned out the Flip Flop financier they had caught was also an informer on the payroll of the Afghan intelligence agency, the National Directorate of Security.

Dishu had been fought over and changed hands several times early on in the war. There was a suspicion that there were spies in the village, and maybe that accounted for the Flip Flops not being quite so active. Whatever the reason was the place was far safer than most villages in the area.

We were given a day off patrol and given camp duty, which consisted of going on stag and various cleaning duties. The day off patrol gave me the chance to write a letter to home and use the satellite phone to give my Nan a ring. The routine at the fort was hard, and it still seemed it would be a very long sixth month tour.

Somebody found a stray cat so we adopted him as our new mascot. We spent a good part of both mornings digging out any small creatures we could find for him and he put on some of the best fights we had ever seen.

Some of the questions the lads asked about Derby were certainly funny. One lad asked what language we spoke in Derby. I thought he was just pulling my leg. He pretended to think that we spoke something like welsh, he said, "I couldn't resist the temptation." Then some soldiers who could barely read and write thought he was asking a serious question and actually meant it.

After two days I was back on patrol again, I was out one night on patrol - which is dangerous at any time. Especially so with the Flip Flops in their current state of jumpy nerves. Odd locals would come out and stare at us. We were never sure if the moment we left they would be on the phone passing on details. These spotters, or "Dickers," were hard to find.

Another daytime patrol was one of the more pleasurable, we had been tasked to go and help do some work rebuilding the local school. I got the job with another Rifleman of building some new football posts. Some of the other lads were tasked with helping to rebuild the school roof that had been damaged by the Flip Flops.

Part of helping the locals with projects was all part of, "Winning the hearts and minds" something that the Brigade were very keen on. We all enjoyed helping out as you really did feel you were doing something positive. We spent most of the day working on various tasks, and it took me a whole day to construct the two goal posts complete with nets.

Everyone let out a cheer when we got the goals into place. With the goalposts up it was followed by a game of football with the local children that we let win. It was the first time since being away; I felt almost human and had a touch of normality. Being on tour almost seemed surreal, and you felt unconnected from the real world. The phone calls home helped immensely, and kept you up to date with what was going on back home. Most importantly, I managed to keep up with the results for Derby County, although that was more often than not depressing in itself!

Back at the fort, it was pizza night, not quite Pizza Hut but they were darn nice all the same. After scoff it was time to get in line for the satellite phone as everyone else made calls to loved ones. One lad had been told by his girlfriend that she was pregnant, too much cheering and banter about who the father was from the lads.

I had already made my peace with my mum and dad before I left for Afghanistan. My girlfriend Helen amazingly was still my girlfriend, even though we had only seen each other a few times in the past nine months.

I had known Helen for years, we went to school together and I suppose we grew up together. We finally got together one night when Helen had been stood up, and not for the first time. She was sitting alone in an Indian restaurant waiting for her date to come. I suppose I used the situation as a lever to finally win her over. I later found out that she had always held a bit of a flame for me. She just thought I had no interest in her. My view was that she always saw me as just a meddling big brother, as opposed to someone she could be interested in romantically.

I wrote to her each and every week, and I had several letters back, which made being in Afghanistan just that little more bearable. She was in a constant state of worry about me, but at the same time proud of what I was doing.

I have heard stories of soldier's wives and girlfriends getting bored and frustrated whilst their men are away, and they end up having affairs. It must be hard to lose someone for six months, not knowing if they will come back injured or alive. Those loved ones left behind have it just as hard as those fighting on the front lines. They are the ones left with the worry and thought at the back of their mind of losing someone dear, each knock at the door could be the one with bad news. The constant media barrage only makes those thoughts become stronger as the death of another soldier is announced or reports of the latest operation.

CHAPTER FIVE

I was proud to just be a rifleman, I had no real ambitions for promotion in the Army. I found that as a rifleman you get bollocked out for anything that goes wrong. Anything and everything gets punished, and it usually ends up with some form of cleaning.

Food is a big part of our lives; it is one of the main topics of conversation. We are motivated by two principals; the first is keeping yourself alive, and the second is killing the enemy. We never stop thinking about food and often say, "When do we next eat?" The words that have been said many times over the years, "An army moves on its stomach" is so true. Food or women were pretty much the favourite topics of conversation, although talking about food only made us hungrier, we yearned for a proper hearty meal. It was this matter of grub that made my life a burden in the fort, I was constantly hungry and some of the food we ate didn't agree with me what so ever, coming out nearly as quickly as it went in.

As often as possible the company cooks are men, who were cooks in civilian life, but not always. Our cook had worked in an Indian restaurant before deciding to join up. He did have a bit of a hot temper at times, and it was not uncommon to see food being thrown at soldiers when he had one of his, "Paddies." Nobody said anything though, as the food he cooked up was good, and his curry night once a fortnight was a real morale lifter. The downside was the smell of dead cow was replaced with the stench of a thousand rotten eggs and garlic as the lads let off their own form of chemical warfare. They even had competitions to see who could give off the most innocuous smell possible.

The only bad food was when we had to eat the 24-hour ration packs, or "Rat" packs. These could be eaten hot or cold, and to be fair were not too bad. I loved the burger, beans, and chocolate pudding. There was no replacement for properly2 cooked food in the cookhouse though.

Our scoff was usually fresh for a few days, followed by canned for a few more, before new supplies came in. One of the biggest supplies was bottled water. This was so we did not have to use the contaminated local supply, which could make a soldier quite ill if they drank it. The bottle water came from a plant at Camp Bastion that got the water from two bore holes, then treated it and even made the bottles for the water to go into.

Many people had asked me what to send me when I was deployed. It had to be a mixture of Haribo, double choc chip cookies and Reggae Reggae sauce. Parcels with food and luxury items were almost the highlight of the tour. Lads would sneak off into a corner to go through the contents and enjoy a taste or two from home.

After the excitement of dodging bullets on patrol, life in the fort could at times seem almost dull. The lads sometimes had too much time to get into mischief. Some even got together one night and put on a show, it was hilarious, with a mixture of crude and black humour.

One thing that did seem to increase on the tour was the smoking; soldiers are great smokers. A packet of fags could last them, with care, about two days. Smoking was a way to pass the time, I think for some it helped to relieve stress and steady the nerves too, seeing as there was a total ban on alcohol.

Another pastime was gambling, but only on a small scale. It too helped to pass the time and add in some excitement. The legality of it was never even thought about. Cards were the mainstay of any gambling. Bets were placed on virtually anything from young James doing another cock up to the number of "Umm's" Meakin would give in his next delivery of orders.

One of the funniest was when one of the lads caught two lizards and decided to have the first annual "Mercian" race. The lizards were named Claridge and Lankin after two of the CO's of the Battalion.

Back out on another night patrol the moon shone bright, and away ahead the silver ribbon of Dishu gleamed for an instant; an ear-splitting crash and a burst of murky, dull-red flame of an IED that had just gone off.

With a larger IED, if the blast hits you directly, you disappear. At a small distance, you may lose a limb or two, and a little farther off you'd suffer shrapnel wounds and a ringing in your ears from the noise of the blast. Just at the edge of the destructive area, the wind of the explosion whistles in your ears, and then sucks back more slowly.

In one IED attack, the Welsh Guards prior to us had lost their commanding officer, a Lt Col Rubert Thorneloe. He was the first commanding officer to be killed in action since the Falklands War. He was diligently checking every spot the convoy was due to move down. Were his Vallon had beeped he thoroughly investigated the source of the beep. He was an officer who would not expect his men to do something he would not do himself. Once checked he climbed back in the Viking and the convoy resumed. Moments later, there was a huge explosion underneath the Vikings rear cab that had had Lt Col Thorneloe sitting on top in. The Viking had run over a low content IED that the Colonel's Vallon must have missed. The area had been cleared not three hours earlier. However, low content IEDs being difficult to detect may have been missed. Other convoys had been up and down the same section since. A Flip Flop must have snuck in seeing the approaching convoy and attached a battery pack.

The explosion caused sheer chaos as the rest of the convoy saw the rear of the Viking lift up into the air and pushed the front cab forward before coming to rest. As the dust and smoke cleared, the devastation and destruction of the rear cab could clearly be seen. It was completely mangled, twisted and partially flattened. Cpl Williams in the front cab had been hit on the head by a large piece if light machine gun that had been blown to bits behind him. Trooper Owen driving the Viking was blown upwards from the driver's seat, his head then impaction on the roof before his face hit the steering wheel on the way down. The Vikings front windscreen was all crazed and cracked from the explosion.

As the rear cab of the Viking filled with dust and debris Cpl Simmons found the door handle but the door was slightly buckled and needed a swift kick to open it. Williams leapt out of his top position and tried to wake Owen up, shouting at him to check his legs. Owen retorted he could feel nothing below his waist and his legs must be gone. Williams shouted at Owen to check them and had found they were both there but may be broken. Williams then jumped from the front cab to the devastated rear cab. Williams knew instantly when he saw Lt Col Thornloe that he had been mortally wounded. The explosion had ripped the floor of the rear cab open, which included the extra blast floor. This had virtually sliced Lt Col Thornloe in two.

The top part of his body had been thrown forward at a 45-degree angle, up against the toolbox, a long container that was often referred to as "the coffin". To Williams it looked as if both of Lt Col Thornloe's legs were missing, he was still conscious though. Williams put a tourniquet on the area where the Colonels left leg had been. By the time Williams had shouted for a second tourniquet the Colonels eyes had rolled back and there was blood oozing from his mouth. Williams checked for a pulse and found nothing; Lt Col Thornloe was gone. Then light flooded the rear cab as another soldier swung the rear door open, another soldier, Harrison, sat opposite covered in dust and suffering from shock. Guardsman Chambers was also still sitting in the rear with shrapnel wounds to his leg. Another, Guardsman Penlington was in a bad way. He and was lying face up. Flesh had been ripped off his left arm, his left leg was bleeding and broken in so many places it was hard to get a grip to drag him out. His leg was completely floppy and was able to move into the strangest of positions, like a piece of bendy rubber. In the end, two soldiers lifted him up and out before giving him a shot of morphine. Trooper Hammond was still missing, and with the Colonel dead Williams fumbled through the dust and darkness trying to find him. He found a hand and tried to grab it, but soon realised it was not attached to an arm. He knew his hopes of finding Williams alive was fading fast. Simmons had run round to see if he could see Hammond, but failing to see anything he knelt down to look at the bottom of the Viking. All he could see was a gaping hole filled with what looked like jelly. This dark red jelly was a mixture of human flesh and body parts. After a while, Hammond's torso was found, missing his arms and legs. Hammond was soon to turn nineteen.

We continued our patrol that was stopped dead after an IED had just gone off and various lads were shouting. As the smoke cleared a solider lay on the ground. A bloody arm lay on the other side of the track. I stood rooted to the spot whilst the rest of the patrol went firm and the medic went in to see what he could do. I got yelled at to go prone and cover the rear of the patrol.

Despite his best efforts the medic knew Rifleman Burns was a gonna, another statistic and the first death of a mate. I had done part of my training with Burns, he was a really jolly chap, always telling bad jokes, but you laughed because they were so bad. At 18, he was the same age as me, had we been in a different order that could have been me.

It really brought home the fact that out here it was not like training or an Xbox game. This was real life and death situations. The Flip Flops job was to see how many of us they could take out.

I don't remember the walk back to the fort, nor the rest of that night. It was as if I was in another world, the loss of Burns had yet to sink in. He would not be the last person we would lose to an IDE.

I was in the lead Mastiff, watching Adams taking pigeon steps on the ground in front of him as he swept the area with his Vallon. As he completed a sweep, he looked to his front as if he had seen something, then he took another small step and the ground erupted beneath him. Even further back, I felt the pressure wave buffet the Mastiff I was in. Then the debris rained down on the roof. As the dust settled we could see half a set of Osprey body armour in the crater left by the IDE, we all feared the worst.

I jumped out of the vehicles with several others and moved towards the crater. It was not long before we were finding body parts and could see flesh hanging in the trees. I tried to pluck up the courage to help a couple of the lads lift Adams body. His head was intact and he had this horrible look on his face. Probably the last look he had before being blown apart. The body still felt warm, he was a well-built lad. Even as just a torso and head was quite a hefty lift for three of us to pick up and get into a black body bag. We got him in and closed his eyes before zipping up the bag, at the same time saying our goodbyes. One of the lads had gone into battle shock and was screaming his head off. A corporal shoved him into the back of a vehicle whilst we got the clean up finished. We made our way back to base in total silence, trying to get our minds around what had happened. For some strange reason it had affected us all more than usual. Maybe we had all seen a little too much death and destruction and were getting to our limits. I know I was reaching my limit, I was unsure of how much more I could take.

Many of the Flip Flops devices were highly unstable. Dealing with them was more akin to Russian roulette. It was common for the Flip Flops, whilst placing or moving IEDs to different locations, to blow themselves up. The Flip Flops often moved devices as they altered their defensive lines or reacted to convoy movements. On one occasion, the controller flying a Predator drone from a base in the Nevada desert spotted a Flip Flop retrieve an IED and then head back to a waiting motorbike. The Predator controller was ready to send in a Hellfire missile as soon as they were both on the motorbike. As the Flip Flop jumped onto the back of the bike, the IED exploded killing both Flip Flops, which saved the US taxpayer the $70,000 cost of a Hellfire missile.

The next day it was as if nothing had happened. The lads were giving their usual banter and seeing who could fart the loudest. This was war, no time to grieve or reflect. We all had a job to do and if our minds went elsewhere, we put everyone at risk. All we had to do was not spot the Flip Flop in the bushes, or the signs of a potential IED, and it could be lights out.

New orders came in that we needed to patrol the ground around the fort at least four times a night. That first night there was one more patrol necessary before daylight. Tired as I was, I volunteered for it.

I went with Corporal Charles. We had only been out some 10 minutes when a machine gun opened up to our left. We got down on our belt buckles and started to crawl. Machine-gun bullets were squealing and snapping overhead pretty much continuously, we had to hug the dirt. It is surprising to see how flat a man can keep and still get along at a good rate of speed.

Then a flare went up and I saw a Flip Flop not forty feet away. The GPMG opened up from the fort and now we had bullets flying over our heads in two directions. I just hoped the lads on the GPMG knew where we were. I tried to lie still and burrow into the dirt at the same time. Nothing happened. The flare died, and Charles gave me a poke in the ribs. We started to crawl on our belt buckles. How we were not seen, I do not know, but we had gone all of one hundred feet before they spotted us. Fortunately, we were on the edge of a shallow hole when the Flip Flops caught our movements so we quickly rolled into the hole. A perfect torrent of bullets ripped up the dirt and cascaded us with gravel and dust. The noise of the bullets whizzing and crackling just a foot or so above us was deafening.

The firing stopped after a bit. I was all for getting out and away immediately. Charles wanted to wait a while. We argued for as much as five minutes. I took matters in my own hands and we got away from there - another piece of luck!

We weren't more than a minute on our way when an explosion went off over the hole we had just been laid up in. Evidently, some bold Flip Flop had chucked something over to make sure of the job, in case the machine guns hadn't worked. It was a narrow escape, two narrow escapes in quick succession. Looking back, I don't think I have ever been more scared. I would have been easy meat if they had decided to rush in and attack us. I can only assume that they feared the fire that would come from the fort as soon as they broke cover.

We made our way back slowly, and eventually the silhouette of the fort came into view. By now, more men had piled out of the fort to come and search for us, fearing the worst. We had been very lucky indeed.

CHAPTER SIX

I want to say a word about patrols because for some reason it fascinated me and was my favourite duty.

If you should be fortunate, or unfortunate enough as the case might be, to be squatting on stag as a lookout, it could be quite a tedious four hours with not much happening. From the top of the fort, you could see a fair distance. In front of the fort, it was mainly some rough tracks with long grass, a few trees and much further, back a wadi which is the Arabic term for a valley, gully or streambed completed the view.

Most times there would be nothing alive visible. The odd animal may cause a rustle in the grass and cause your heart to race. Every once in a while, a loud bang would be heard far off in the distance as another IED was set off. Not sure if IEDs actually killed more animals than they did people. However, cattle wandering down roads would often fall victim to an IED. Maybe the Loggie bomb squad should have been employing cows to find IEDs, they seemed damn good at it. For most cows it was a mooving experience, in more ways than one! I promise that will be my first and last bad joke.

Ordinarily, there is little movement to be seen, yet you know that not too far away Flip Flops were planning their next move.

After dark was the usual time for the Flip Flops to try and get as close as possible, either to gather intelligence, let off a few mortars or plant IEDs. Our job was to try to prevent them operating in the area and protect Dishu.

Most of our patrols go out armed and equipped lightly. In some areas, we have to move softly, and at times very quickly. You never knew what was lurking in the distance - random machine gun fire would often open up and everyone would go to ground, trying to spot where it had come from.

Some patrols were supposed to avoid encounters with Flip Flop patrols. These ones were to try to gather intelligence, to recce an area for a later attack. Usually these patrols were much smaller, maybe just four of the lads. Every patrol, as well as our SA80 and combat kit, we took plenty of water as you could dehydrate very fast, especially with the weight of all the body armour and ammunition. You took at least six fully loaded magazines, some rations and any extra kit you had been asked to carry.

On a night patrol, you would stare constantly through the darkness and get to the point where you could see almost as well as a cat. On recce patrols you need to avoid being seen at all costs. You had neither the firepower nor manpower to take on the Flip Flops. British Army doctrine has always worked on the four to one ratio to win a firefight.

The Flip Flops patrolled quite haphazardly, sometimes alone and sometimes in pairs, but did also like small groups. One man leads and the others follow to the rear. They never seemed covert with their patrols, but then the Flip Flops much preferred either to ambush or lay IEDs. Most of the patrols that were seen were usually out to lay IEDs. They always seemed to carry an RPG and a PK machine gun, and often looked a ragged bunch. Like in Vietnam, the Flip Flops easily blended in with the locals. Making it hard at times to tell who was friend and who was foe.

I was out one night with another man, prowling in the dark, when I encountered an Afghan boy who was alone. He was quite a way from any house or villages. It was hard to tell if he was just out wandering or doing some spying for the Flip Flop's. Children made very unsuspecting intelligence gatherers and could easily be turned to the "Cause." The use of 'dickers' was all too common, and they would use mobile phones, mirrors or even kites to alert the Flip Flops. The funny part about using kites was that the Taliban had originally banned them.

The look of hate this boy had in his eyes towards us took me aback a little. The interpreter tried to talk to him, but he was very guarded, and pretty much refused to speak

After a while, we separated and the boy went on his way. We had no reason to detain him and could not force him to come back with us. We tried out best to talk to him and say it was for his own safety. I think he would have rather been shot than be seen with British soldiers.

An hour or so later the sky started to turn from black to blue, and it was evident that dawn was near. We were under a mile away from the Fort when we saw the boy again. Had he been following our every move all this time? Were we about to be ambushed?

All the lad's became even more alert as we walked down the track, eyes peeled on all sides looking for any movement. Nothing happened and we got safely back to the fort. I think the fear of the unknown is often worse than the actual event, I did feel physically sick once I got into the fort. All the lads spoke of what had happened, and the Sergeant went to report what had happened to the OC.

The rest of us stayed up to have breakfast before getting our heads down for a few hours' sleep.

Once I was out on patrol, I was lying down at the time, a flare went up and one of the lads bizarrely was standing up. I had no idea why the hell he was standing up whilst everyone else was crouched down. He had frozen and stayed that way until the flare died, but I realised he was not one of our lads but a Flip Flop.

When the darkness settled again, I got to my feet and jumped at him. Going into the clinch, I missed him with the butt of my rifle and lost my grip on it, leaving the weapon dangling by the sling. He struck at me with his automatic, which I think he must have dropped, though I'm not sure of that. Anyway, we fell into each other's arms and went at it barehanded. I got under the ribs and tried to squeeze the breath out of him, but he was like a snake that could curl round you.

At the same time, I felt that he didn't relish the clinch. I slipped my elbow up and got under his chin, forcing his head back. His breath smelled. I was choking him when he brought his knee up and got me in the stomach, and again on the instep when he brought his heel down.

By now, the rest of the patrol had realised what was happening and came to my aid. They wrestled with him and got him to his feet. We had our first prisoner and bagged a Flip Flop. He would be questioned, then processed through the Afghan legal system to see if any criminal charges could be brought.

I felt pleased with myself, at the same time I was blasted by the Sergeant for being so stupid, putting my life at risk. With the bollocking finished, he did congratulate me for the successful outcome.

He was on his own and had either got lost or was out putting IEDs down. Although he had no sign of any bombs on him, he did test positive for explosives when we used our field test kit.

We would often use a wadi and natural trenches for cover. I slipped down the slight incline into the wadi, and presently found myself in a little valley. The grass was rank and high, sometimes nearly up to my chin, and the ground was slimy and treacherous.

We were heading towards a bridge to check for IED's and the only safe way to approach was from the wadi itself. We finally made it to the bridge and sent a poor Sapper, Army slang for engineer, to check the supports for anything suspicious. An IED had never been found in this area but if the Flip Flops blew it up they would harm their supply route as well as ours, well that was the theory anyhow.

I got back into the grass and made my way downstream. Sliding gently through the grass, I kept catching my feet on something hard that felt like roots; but there were no trees in the neighbourhood. The roots turned out to be the bones of cattle that had collected there over many years. Looking into the water, I could see the skull of a goat, I think.

After getting out of the bones, we moved downstream and heard the low voices of Afghan farmers or possibly Flip Flops in the distance. Creeping to the edge of the grass, I peeped out. I could dimly make out the forms of two men standing with some cattle around them. They did look more like farmers than Flip Flops, and we decided not to alert them to our presence and continued on our way.

Some patrols were almost routine, even though done in different order, we would often re-visit the same area on a regular basis. We would often provide cover for the Sappers to do their checks for IEDs, although a couple of the lads had been trained to clear IEDs as well.

Sometimes the Flip Flops would lay an IED reasonably near the surface, which was easy to spot and remove. You would constantly look for the telltale signs of fleshly disturbed earth or objects or shapes that didn't look natural.

An IED, also known as a roadside bomb, is basically an explosive that is planted in locations that will cause death or injury. They may be constructed from conventional military explosives, such as an artillery round, which is then attached to some form of detonating mechanism. IEDs in Afghanistan have caused over 66% of the coalition casualties so far.

The British Army first used the term Improvised Explosive Device in the1970s, after the Provisional Irish Republican Army (IRA) used bombs made of Semtex, smuggled from Libya, and agricultural fertilizer to make highly effective booby trap devices or remote-controlled bombs. An IED is designed to be destructive and can incorporate lethal, noxious, pyrotechnic, or incendiary chemicals that are designed to destroy or incapacitate personnel or vehicles. In some cases, IEDs are used to disrupt or delay troop movements in Afghanistan. They are also a good way to set up an ambush, an IED will stop the convoy or troop movement in its tracks. IEDs can incorporate military or commercially sourced explosives; some are even made with homemade explosives. An IED is usually made from five main components: a switch (activator), an initiator (fuse), container (body), charge (explosive), and finally a power source (battery). An IED designed for use against armoured targets, such as APC (Armoured Personnel Carriers) or even tanks has to be designed for armour penetration, by using what is called a shaped charge or an explosively formed penetrator. IEDs can be extremely diverse in terms of design and can make use of items found lying about the house or garage. IEDs designed for antipersonnel, typically also contain some form of shrapnel, such as nails or ball bearings, which was known as "shipyard confetti" by the IRA as the shrapnel was usually scrap metal found in shipyards.

Various methods, from remote control pressure-sensitive bars or trip wires to infrared magnetic triggers, can be used to trigger an IED. In some cases, multiple IEDs have been wired together in a daisy chain to attack a convoy of vehicles that are spread out. The majority of IEDs we came across were the pressure sensitive type, and whilst not always well put together they were well designed.

Many IEDs are very unstable and prone to exploding without being activated. This has caused death or serious injury to many of the people making and planting IEDs.

The British approach to IEDs is to isolate the device and then use a specialist team to defuse it. This is a painstaking process that could take three hours or more per device, which slows a convoy or troop movement right down. In turn leading to a high potential for an ambush. The American approach is to blow them up in place, as fast as possible. Americans also had ground-penetrating radar to detect them, which could even detect low metal content devices, which the British metal detector is unable to locate.

On another patrol, we halted the patrol at the end of a wall and waited. Air support had been called in to take out a compound that had been firing at the patrol. However, we could not get a proper location on the source so had to call in a bombing run. Then along came a deep rumble that shook the ground, with a dull boom. A spurt of blood-red flame squirted up our near side, and a rolling column of grey smoke.

Then another rumble and the area in front of the compound seemed to open up and move slowly skyward with a world-wrecking, soul-paralysing crash. A murky red glare lit up the smoke screen and against it a mass of tossing-up debris, for an instant I thought I saw the black silhouette of a whole human body spread-eagled and spinning like a pinwheel. However, it was just my mind playing tricks.

Most of the patrol, even at that distance, was knocked down by the gigantic impact of the explosion. A shower of earth and rock chunks fell around us.

We had six casualties from shock and wounds among men who were supposed to be at a safe distance from the bombing. The F16 had dropped its first bomb a little bit too short. Most of the patrol had been caught by the blast. Blue on blue, as it was called, was not that common, but there was always the chance of being too close to air support as it went in. On this occasion, we were in the right place and the F16 pilot dropped his bomb too short. The Flip Flops must have escaped as the second bomb that hit the target flattened it. We found no human remains just a dead goat.

CHAPTER SEVEN

I do think ours was a just cause, to try to give the Afghan people the safety to go about their daily lives, without fearing the Flip Flops. The other important part was to continue the war against terrorism. On paper, it seemed very noble indeed. However, being in the midst of it, 'The Cause' sometimes just did not seem worth the loss of life on either side, or the civilians caught up in the middle.

Modern warfare is fought as much by the politicians as it is by the soldier.

The cause of the war in Afghanistan is based in history. Following the Soviet withdrawal from Afghanistan in 1989, and the fall of the Afghan Communist government in 1992, a lengthy civil war raged on between the various factions of anti-Communist Afghan fighters, who called themselves the Mujahidin.

In this realm of chaos, Mullah Mohammed Omar was seen as a new an upcoming leader by some former Mujahedeen. He was himself a former mujahedin fighter who returned to his home village after the fall of the Communist regime. He then led a new armed group called the Taliban. The Taliban actually means 'student' and many of the original recruits to Omar's new movement were Islamic religious students. Other former mujahedin leaders of Pashtun background began to join with the Taliban as this new group wanted to impose their own form of law and order Afghanistan. They wanted to impose an extreme version of Islamic law. Under this extreme Taliban led Islamic law that was imposed on the local populous, men are expected to grow beards and attend religious services regularly, women are not allowed to work outside the home or attend school. Television is banned, and religious minorities had to wear clothing that could identify them as 'non-Muslim'. Then in 2001 as well as attracting the support of Osama bin Laden and his Al-Qaida organisation they ordered the destruction of all non-Islamic idols and statues in areas under their control.

Through the autumn of 2001 the Taliban continued to put pressure on the Northern Alliance. This pressure was often with the aid of

Osama bin Laden and his Arab forces. Then on September 9th 2001, the Northern Alliance leader Ahmad Shah Massoud was mortally wounded in an assassination attempt. The attempt was carried out by two Arab men posing as journalists. This attack was the work of Al-Qaida and was a possible prelude to the airline hijackings and terrorism that occurred in the United States on September 11th. The Northern Alliance responded to Massoud's killing with an aerial attack on Kabul on the night of September 11th.

The killing of Massoud was coordinated with the terror attacks on the United States that took place on September 11, which many saw as significant as the attack on Pearl Harbour on December 7, 1941. As the United States laid blame for the attacks on Al-Qaida and Osama Bin Laden, they began to formulate plans to take the fight to Al-Qaida and its Taliban sponsors in Afghanistan. Which was the start of Americas Global War on Terror.

After we had completed three of our six-month tour we were indeed battle hardened. However, I still felt like a novice with much to learn. The first 3 months had been hard, adjusting to the hot climate and getting use to patrols. Slowly becoming aware of what was going on and I suppose situational awareness. The training I received did help, but no training in the world gives you the same feeling of terror as when you first come under effective enemy fire. Nor does it ready you for the sights or the smell after a fellow soldier has been blown to bits by an IED. The sight of a human corpse, or one that has been blown apart with body parts hanging from tree branches, the head blown onto the roof of a compound, these images are etched into my mind, I will never be able to get rid of them. I have already had to fill more body bags than I thought possible and we were only half way through the tour.

The knight of the middle Ages was all dressed up like a hardware store with about a hundred pounds of armour. However, he rode a horse and had a squire or some such striker, trailing along in the rear with the things to make him comfortable when the fighting was over.

The modern soldier gets very little help with his war making. He is, in fact, more likely to be helping somebody else than asking for assistance for himself. He has to carry about eighty pounds of weight with him all the time.

He has entrenching tools, a bayonet, a water bottle, a mess kit, a rifle, ammunition and magazines, weapon cleaning kit, all of which is draped, hung, and otherwise disposed over his body by means of webbing. In the intense heat, water in quite large amounts is another essential that adds further to the weight, and limits your ability to manoeuvre quickly. A modern soldier parallels the old-time knight only in the matter of the helmet and the rifle, which, with the bayonet, corresponds to the lance, sword, and battle-axe; three in one. Although at times, the horses of old are replaced by a Jackal or Viking.

The modern soldier carries all his possessions with him all the time. He hates to yomp.

I remember very vividly that first day. The temperature was around 110 degrees, and it had been arranged that we would start our patrol at twelve noon, the very worst time of the day in terms of heat.

Before we had gone five miles we all began to wilt, we weren't use to the heat yet. I was already touched with flu and was way under par. That did not make any difference, I still had to carry on and wilt a bit more.

Our weapons weighed nearly 5Kg or 6.58Kg if you were the unlucky one to carry the LSW (Light Support Weapon) which had a slightly longer barrel and tripod legs at the front.

The SA80 assault rifle originally entered service in 1985, replacing the SLR as the British forces standard assault rifle. The SA80 takes standard NATO 5.56x45mm ammunition, with a magazine capacity of 30 rounds. The SA80 and its ammunition were designed to be lighter and more ergonomic than its predecessor the SLR. Most SA80s used on the front line, like the ones we had as infantry, have SUSAT scopes, making for an accurate weapon. However, the weapon was a pig to clean. In fact, the SAS and SBS rejected the SA80 in favour of the M16, and later the C8 Carbine. Given the chance, the Para's and Marines would swap their SA80 for an M16 or C8.

Once in the field, it wasn't long before some problems became apparent with the SA80. Soldiers found that the gun would jam or magazines would drop out of their rifles without warning. This was found to be due to the exposed magazine clip, so a modification was put in place with a raised ring of metal around the magazine clip. The weapon was prone to jamming due to the number of working parts and its thirst for gun oil. Use of the SA80 in extreme climates showed up further shortcomings, the plastic components in very hot or cold climates would often fail. In Sierra Leone, 2000, during various operations members of the Pathfinder Platoon discovered that the safety catches on their SA80s were failing in the heat, rendering their weapon useless. The SA80 is also a heavy gun, almost 1kg heavier than similar 5.56mm assault rifles.

The SA80 has now become the SA80 A2 after having been extensively modified by Heckler & Koch. The A2 addresses some, if not all of the shortcomings of the SA80. The main one being 'stoppages' along with its poor reliability, especially in hot and dusty environments. Much of the work carried out consisted of coating many of the 'working parts' with a Teflon coating. Some of the lads still moan about the SA80, mainly the fact that it is a pain in the arse, especially when compared to the simpler and more reliable C8 that the SAS and American forces use. The SA80 though, is one of the most accurate rifles in service today. The MK2 version is much less prone to stoppages and works well most of the time. The SA80 needs plenty of gun oil to stay fit and healthy, the downside with oil is that it attracts dirt and this leads to even more cleaning.

The blast caught us off guard on a cool Sunday morning, as we were drinking tea in the courtyard of the fort. The door to our fort suddenly flew open and two lads came running in off stag, they pointed out the nearby plume of white smoke. It had been a quiet morning so far. The Afghan locals were at prayers in the local mosque. Without much information or time to get fully kitted up, we quickly threw on our gear and moved towards where the plume of smoke was coming from with the platoon Sergeant leading. We knew it was most likely to be a Flip Flop attack, but we had no idea how bad it was.

We heard from an Afghan who topped as we were on patrol, that a suicide bomber had killed several people in Dishu near to a mosque, and quite a few were wounded. Within minutes of us arriving nearby the local police arrived and began to shoot wildly in anger. The problem was their shoots were a bit too near to our heads, which convinced everyone that we were putting ourselves in danger trying to help out. We needed backup and we needed it fast. The Sergeant called for the rest of the platoon to be ready, as well as the Royal Marines in the next patrol base to us, to come and give us a dig out. The blast was far enough away to make for a dangerous walk through a now-panicked street, so we returned to the safety of the compound until reinforcements arrived. In these situations, we could well be sitting ducks as the Flip Flops made good use of the confusion to take a few soldiers out. In the melee, it would be hard to work out which were locals and which were Flip Flops, the local dickers would alert the Flip Flops to our presence anyhow.

It was not long before the first casualty appeared at our gates. It was a kid with a head injury and there had not been any more space at the local medical centre. We had to make an assessment on his condition before deciding if he would need evacuating out of the area by helicopter, we had a Chinook standing by as serious casualties were expected.

It took over an hour for the Royal Marines and their transport to arrive before we could go back into Dishu, assess the casualties, and help the local populous. The Marines would be our guard and would put up a perimeter leaving us free to help in any way we could.

On arrival at the bombsite, we rolled our sleeves up, and put on blue latex gloves.

A rather battered Ambulance was already at the scene. Dented and abused after years of service in a war zone. The back was open to reveal a young looking boy lying down on a stretcher, his naked body was covered with a brown cloth blanket. He looked about sixteen. The interior of the ambulance was covered in blood that had not been cleaned off. The boy lying on the stretcher had his head covered by a mass of bandages, which had ended up looking like a large gauze egg. His skull seemed to now have unnatural shape and size to it.

He already had a drainage tube in his nose and an IV line was running right into his left hand via a cannula. A local man was crouching beside him, holding the drip in one hand and the boys very pale hand in the other. The boy's eyes were half-open and he just managed to follow my finger when I moved it across his face. He was moaning slightly, his body shivering from the shock of what I expect was serious fluid loss. I placed my gloved hand on his shoulder in an attempt to reassure him and to add a little warmth. He was very thin and lacked any body tone or muscle. He was a teenager that looked so childlike and so delicate.

The Corporal I was with was a battlefield first aider, so he cut the medical tape and began to unwrap the gauze to see if he could do anything further. I cradled the boy's neck with my arms across his collarbone and my hands under his head. Our faces were intimately close and his sad eyes, which to me looked close to death, looked up at me and made me want to cry. I don't remember any smells. I don't remember anything but the boy's face and feeling him shiver as life slowly ebbed away from him. I could feel the wetness of the blood through my gloves on the back of his neck. As the gauze came off it revealed a mass of absorbent pads that were basically holding in his damaged brain. The decision was made to not remove any more layers of bandage as it was clear they had reddish-pink brain matter on them. We knew he did not have long left, and all we could do was make him as comfortable as possible. Part of his skull had been shattered and pushed into his brain; it was a small miracle that he was still alive. We still called in for an immediate medevac just in case there was the slimmest of chances that he could survive.

The boy had been seated on a motorcycle no more than five meters from where the suicide bomber had detonated. He had just passed by at the wrong time and became an unfortunate victim of circumstance.

My hands were coated in blood and shaking. I knew his chances were slim, if nothing, and he may well pass away before the helicopter even got here. Other casualties had been found so it was not a wasted journey. I felt so helpless; there was nothing more I could do but offer comfort to a dying teenager.

The lads who had remained to help, got the pleasure of removing the completely pulverised remains of the suicide bomber, along with three other casualties, who were also dismembered and difficult to visualise as human beings, such was the destruction of the blast. Hands, legs, arms and feet had been blown off in all directions adding to the horror.

The image of that boy dying in my arms still haunts me to this day; he was just an innocent victim, in the wrong place at the wrong time. As soldiers, we knew that death was an unwanted part of the job, even though we try not to dwell on it. Being at war meant casualties were inevitable, but that still never made it any easier to come to terms with.

CHAPTER EIGHT

The conditions we had to grin and bear were nothing like those who fought in World War 1 trenches. I remember reading an extract about a soldier in the trenches during my basic training.

"Later in the summer I came down with a case of trench fever.

This disease occurs due to us to remaining for long periods in water and mud, not helped with sleeping in the foul air of the dugouts that is our accommodation on the front line. The chief symptom is a high temperature, and aches throughout my body, very much like a flu. With trench fever, I was deemed unsuitable to be on the frontline and sent back to a place in Arras and spent a week recovering from my illness.

When I had recovered from the fever, I re-joined my battalion in the Somme district at a place called Mill Street. This was in reality just a series of trenches along a road only a short distance behind our second lines, but still in range of German artillery.

Within an hour of my arrival, a German gas shell was deposited on us, the gas was new at the time and called tear gas. The unpleasant gas in the shells, whilst comparatively harmless compared to mustard gas was still unpleasant. When you got a good lungful you choked, and your eyes began to run. If your exposed skin got wet the gas would cause it to sting like hell. There was no controlling the tears and the effects lasted for quite a time, rendering you unable to fight back. The goggles we were provided with for this gas were nearly useless; we all resorted to using the regular gas helmet that proved effective against the gas.

The gas mask was a horrid thing to have to wear for any length of time. It restricted your breathing and the strong smell of rubber left a bitter aftertaste in your mouth, long after you had taken the gas mask off.

The sheer amount of death and dead bodies were enough to give you nightmares. I had never seen so many before, just piled up on one another. You could not walk very far before spotting another and another. They were all over the place, both Germans and our own.

There were arms and legs sticking out of the mud in any crater that had been the last place they stood. You could easily tell what nationality they were by their uniforms.

Sometimes a corpse would seem to follow you with his eyes wide open gaze. We would do our best to cover them up or turn them over offering at least some dignity.

The smell here was horrific, a frightful and sickening smell that strikes one in the face. You could not escape the smell and it remained in your nostrils nearly all the time."

Now being in a war zone myself, I could relate to that narrative, although we did not have to worry about the gas that was replaced with IEDs, and damp smelly trenches were replaced by a smelly cowshed. Thankfully, the death toll was on a minuscule scale compared to that of World War 1. The thing about war is people die on all sides. However, even with a 100 year gap it was bizarre to find the same thoughts and feelings as a modern soldier. Our equipment and protection may be better, and survival rates higher, but we all lived with the same fears and were doing the same job.

One of the closest calls I had in all of my deployment was totally unrelated to the Flip Flops.

Several of the lads, including myself, were squatted around a mess tin getting a brew on, when there was a terrific explosion. Investigation proved that an unexploded IED had been buried where we had set up our mess tins and got the water on the boil, it had gone off as the heat penetrated the ground. That IED must have been missed when the Fort was checked by the Sappers over 12 months ago.

After that, I was told I was banned from using my mess tin to make a brew and asked why I had just not gone and used the Burco in the Cookhouse.

The point that hit home for me is that we were never truly safe and we were foreigners in a foreign land. That hid so many surprises from the years of fighting. I still got ribbed that I had planted the IED so I could be injured and sent home.

It seemed to be a hidden wish that the lads would get wounded and sent home early. Some were not "Out there," because they wanted to be, but because they had to be. They will fight like a bag of wildcats when they get where the fighting is, but at the same time, no one is going around looking for trouble.

When the lads got letters from home and found out that the wife, the children, or the old mother was sick, he wants to go home. So a couple put in their time hoping for a wound that would be "Cushy" enough to mean being sent to Camp Bastion, and then being sent back to the fort. We all had times when we just wanted to go home. However, you just took the rough with the smooth and found ways to survive mentally.

One of the lads in my section, Rifleman Marshall was desperate to get home to see his newborn. He was no fighting man and didn't pretend to be, and he didn't care who knew it. I was amazed he made it all the way through training only to realise he didn't want to fight. He was determined to get a wound that meant he could be sent home.

One morning as we were preparing to go on patrol and the lads were a little jumpy and nervous, I heard a shot behind me, and a bullet chugged into the sandbags beside me. I whirled around, my first thought being that we were being shot at.

It was Marshall. He had been monkeying with his rifle and had shot himself in the hand. Of course, Marshall was at once under suspicion of a self-inflicted wound. However, the suspicion was removed instantly. Marshall was hopping around screaming his head off.

"Oh shit Oh shit, part of my finger is gone."

The poor lad was so mortified over the loss of part of his finger, and no one could accuse him of shooting himself intentionally.

CHAPTER NINE

Day dawned, and a small breeze from the west scattered the dust on the tracks around the fort. There was not a cloud in sight and the sun shone bright.

We made final kit preparations that morning. Then at around nine o'clock Captain Green gave us a little talk that confirmed our suspicions, that the day was going to consist of a large operation.

He said, as nearly as I can remember:

"Lads, I want to tell you that there is to be one of the most important operation undertaken in Afghanistan so far, and one the most important one we have undertaken so far."

Operation Moshtarak as it was called, which was an offensive to disrupt the production and supply of Opium in the area, that is best described as the "poppy-growing belt". The Opium trade was big business and was an essential income for the Taliban to fund more weapons and explosives in order to aid their cause.

Helmand Province is the largest opium-growing province within Afghanistan, accounting for nearly 42% of Afghanistan's total opium production. Afghanistan itself accounts for 30% of the world's production. The United Nations Office of Drugs and Crime described the irrigated areas of Helmand as pretty much ideal for yielding high opium poppy cultivation. They estimate that 70,000 hectares in the Province are now being cultivated for poppy growing. They also estimate that they are between 1,000–1,500 small opium traders and between 300-500 larger traders

The main target of the offensive was widely considered to be Marja (also Marjah or Marjeh), which had been controlled for years by Flip Flop militants as well as drug traffickers. Afghan troops were given a lead role in the ground forces, comprising of about 60% of the attacking troops.

We were to be with other British, American and Canadian forces in the Nad-e-Ali district. On the 9th February two Para's had been killed in the same area. They had died whilst on patrol after both being fatally shot and were from 3rd Battalion Parachute Regiment and the 4th Battalion Parachute Regiment.

That incident had put everyone on an even higher state of alert. We all knew we were going into a proper war zone and would be working alongside the Afgan National Army. Working with the Afghan National Army brought in a mixture of views. Some of the lads thought they were just farmers with guns, whilst the higher ranking officers saw them as essential to nurture and train, mainly so they could take control and let the coalition forces go home, leaving Afghanistan to manage itself, although that looks and feels quite some time away.

Early in the morning of the first day of Operation Moshatrak over15, 000 UK, U.S. and Afghan troops were dropped into Marjah and Nad-e-Ali by helicopter. We were dropped in slightly later in Nad-e- Ali, along with Afghan troops.

Not far into the battle, a British soldier from another battalion was killed by an explosion in Nad-e- Ali, although resistance did seem quite light initially.

Flip Flops gave the excuse or propaganda that it was to reduce civilian casualties. A lot of Afghan people had already fled the area after becoming aware of the impending attack.

At eleven thirty o'clock the initial fire support let loose – I saw the most intense bombardment of artillery and mortar fire I had even seen. It seemed like guns from all sides of the coalition were blasting the hell out of various targets before we were to move in.

The noise form all the explosions made my eardrums ache, I thought I would go mad if the noise did not stop soon. I must admit I was quite nervous and scared, but tried my best not to show it. I think everyone tried to conceal their nervousness, even though inside they may be dying with fright

I could see that the faces of the lads were hard-set and pale. Some of them looked positively green. They smoked cigarette after cigarette, lighting the new ones on the butts of the old ones.

All through the bombardment, the Flip Flops seemed comparatively quiet. Probably, they were holed up in areas we were unaware of.

Intelligence could be very good at times and very sketchy in others. Flip Flops were a slippery bunch and very good at the kind of Guerrilla warfare they were involved in.

I looked into the distance and wondered if I would survive. There were moments when I felt distinctly sorry for myself and wondered how and why I had got myself to this point.

The time, strangely enough went fast. Was this how the World War 1 soldiers felt as they awaited in the trenches for the order to "Go over the top" and into no man's land to meet their fate.

We made ourselves ready for the order to move once artillery had done its job. We had tank support as well as light armour; they were always a welcoming sight.

Some of the lads gave their bayonets a quick check to make sure they were secure, and I looked to my bolt action to see that it worked well and my magazine was attached properly. I had thirty rounds in the magazine, and I didn't intend to rely too much on the bayonet. At a few seconds to twelve, I looked at my wrist watch, and as we awaited the order to move in I was afflicted again with that empty feeling in my stomach. Without too much time to dwell or think, the order was given to move forward and clear the area.

The terrain was level out to the point where the little hill with a few trees was the only feature that broke up the long grass that led to a group of buildings. We had no idea how effective the artillery had been.

Warrior tanks moved forward to pick up any targets, these tanks were ideal for Afghanistan. They were classed as a light tank and quite small and mobile. They were also used to give us protection when travelling to various operations. Although at Dishu everything was done on foot.

They had done their job well so far, with only 22 soldiers being killed whilst travelling in a Warrior in Afghanistan.

I loved the noise they made due to the roar of the 550Hp V8 Condor engine. Although I cannot say, it was quite so nice to be sitting in one with the noise and the ability of the tank to bounce around on rough terrain. I am sure if you did not wear your helmet in the back you would quite easily be knocked unconscious as your head bounced off the roof.

The Warrior was developed by GKN Defence, and a total of 789 were manufactured between 1987 and 1995 for the British Army. The Army has recently had its Warriors upgraded to extend its service life. The upgrade, as well as various reliability and performance upgrades, included the addition of the General Dynamics UK Bowman tactical communications system, and a night fighting capability in the form of the Thales Optronics battle group thermal imaging system. A new turret and stabilised 40mm cannon will be fitted to 449 Warriors.

The Battle Group Thermal Imaging (BGTI) includes an eyesafe laser rangefinder, GPS / inertial navigation system, thermal imager and fire control system, making the Warrior much more formidable.

The tanks were just ahead of us and lumbered along in an imposing row. They lurched down into dips and then pulled out again, tipped and bounced as they made their way across the smooth looking terrain. The long grass hid the fact that the terrain was full of holes and dips that made for hard going on foot.

Some sporadic fire did start as we got closer and the Warriors retaliated with their 30mm RARDEN cannon and 7.62mm machine gun.

As we moved in closer, we used the tank for protection by moving up behind it. Then suddenly a rocket was fired from a building, which made its way to a tank on our far right. The explosion rocked the tank violently but the appliqué armour had done its job and protected the tank. It quickly backed up, still surrounded by smoke from the blast - as other w

Warriors opened up on the location that the rocket had come from.

We continued to move forward. I thought we must be nearly there as the Warriors had held back to give us covering fire so we could move in to sweep the buildings and flush out any remaining Flip Flops.

There was sporadic gunfire, but as soon as it opened up the Warriors fired more 30mm shells and it was subdued for a period of time. We were now going to be doing what was called "House to house" fighting otherwise known as, "FIBUA" (Fighting In A Built Up Area). We had to clear each building before moving on to the next. This sort of fighting could be very hard, you could not see round corners or know if any booby traps had been laid, or what lay behind the next door.

I followed Sergeant Page into the first building, as he entered he swept the room with his rifle and I followed in covering his rear. We made our way through three small rooms before moving upstairs. It was quite dark inside and even a shadow could make you jump. I tried to stay as calm as I could, and that's no easy feat. I just felt like turning around and running straight out the front door. We cleared the building and made our way outside to hear the sound of several SA80's letting rip. Obviously, another group had hit the jackpot.

At the end of my participation in the battle I wasn't wounded. Quite a number of Flip Flops had been killed, and a good haul of weapons and rockets had been recovered. We even found a stash of raw opium, the main factor in the setting up of operation Moshatrak.

We did take a few prisoners. Meakin grabbed me and turned one over to me. We searched him rapidly, and applied plastic ties to his wrists. He did not look very happy and if looks could kill…

As we hurried back towards the Warriors that would now take us out of the area, I heard more explosions in the distance but could not work out if these were from the coalition or the Flip Flops. I have never been so glad to be in the back of the Warrior, it was extremely hot, but just nice to sit down and feel safe.

Going back we did come under some fire, and we could hear the turret mounted 7.62 machine gun blasting away. We also heard the odd ping as a bullet bounced off the tanks amour. Apache helicopters could be heard coming in to finish off any final resistance and give us some cover.

After getting my prisoners back to the rear, I came up again but couldn't find my battalion. I threw in with a battalion of Australians and was with them for twenty-four hours.

We had not suffered any casualties and I think that was mainly down to the Warriors providing cover, and of course that element of luck.

The net result of the battle was that we had not only got rid of a Flip Flop stronghold but also disrupted a piece of their supply chain. To us a good result was always to return home without any casualties, even if we had not had any form of contact.

For weeks after our battle at Nad-e-Ali the Warriors and the Flip Flops who had been shot dead by the lads inside a building was the chief topic of conversation in our platoon.

Our participation in Operation Moshatrak had been a success and the report we got back was from the OC was:

On the morning of February 14th, 2010, a report in a newspaper had the headline, "Opium City Taken Back"

"After British, American and Afghan troops seized crucial positions, after overwhelming the immediate resistance, they encountered an intense but sporadic firefight unfolded as they began house-to-house searches. According to American commanders, the troops had achieved all the intended first-day objectives, which included advancing into the city itself in order to seize strategic points like government buildings and one of the city's bazaars in the centre. The following door to door search for weapons and insurgents was expected to last around five days if not more, with the possibility of hundreds of bombs and IEDs laying hidden in houses and on roads and footpaths that would need to be cleared."

On the second day of the operation, it was reported that British troops had pushed through Showal, a town that for the last two years that had been under the control of insurgents. They had used it as a staging post to build IEDs and to train their fighters to plant them. In other raids, explosives for numerous IEDs were seized. They seized not only bomb-making equipment, but also drug processing chemicals. Drugs were also found and seized in surrounding fields belonging to Opium farmers. Among the drugs seized were 74 tons of opium poppy seeds, 17 tons of black tar opium, 400 pounds of hashish and 443 pounds of heroin.

Sadly, twelve civilians, with ten of them from the same family, were killed when their houses were struck by two rockets, fired by an Allied

Rocket launcher. It was reported however, that the rockets were on target and the house had been used by the Taliban for staging attacks on Allied forces."

CHAPTER TEN

With Operation Moshatrak a success, we went back to the routine of patrols and bonding with the locals. The OC would hold fortnightly meetings with the village elders to see what we could do to help them. It was a two way process, as this in turn built up trust that meant we would gain vital intelligence of what the Flip Flops were up to in our area.

It must have been a few days after our attack in Nad -e-Ali that Captain Green had me up and told me that I would be promoted once we returned to the UK.

The Captain said that in the course of the attack I proved my worth and I had shown leadership potential. I would become a Lance Corporal, which was the first rung on the promotion ladder.

I did protest that the honour was maybe slightly premature, and that I really didn't think I was good enough. I was worried that I still felt like a rookie and not up to the dizzy heights of leadership. But then I have never been one to take compliments.

In spite of my feelings in the matter, I accepted the decision cheerfully, even though I was worried I was being promoted before I was ready. I managed to convey the impression to Captain Green that I was greatly elated, and I looked forward to taking on the responsibilities of a Lance Corporal. I had also lacked confidence at school and shied away from anything that looked too hard. Maybe it was a weakness, but I was more than happy to coast along.

I was preparing for out next patrol, we had been briefed by Captain Green - it all sounded very simple for a change.

The whole thing sounded as simple as ABC. All we had to do was go over there and get rid of the enemy. The captain did not say how many Flip Flops could be there, nor what they would be doing while we were taking their comfortable little position. Indeed, he seemed to quite carelessly leave the Flip Flops out of the reckoning. I am not sure if Captain Green did not want to spook us or the intelligence had said this was a soft target. Everything seemed to have a casual air about it.

Had the Flip Flops really moved out of the area? Were we just mopping up what was left?

At Three-thirty in the morning we were ready, stripped to just the lightest necessary equipment. As it was a quick hit and run affair, the objective was to be back by breakfast.

Lieutenant Meakin took us out and we made way to our position that was within a mile of the fort. We walked in extended line but in the strictest silence for about half a mile. By now we were all very familiar with the area, and could of almost made our way blind folded. I did enjoy the night patrols more so than the daytime patrols. Partly because of the heat, but I suppose night time patrols just seemed more exciting somehow.

After we had gone about a mile, Meakin gave the signal to lie down. We lay still half an hour or so and then crawled forward.

We crawled along for about ten minutes, and Meakin passed the word in whispers to get ready, as we were nearly on them. Each of us made sure our weapons were set. It was fairly still. Away off to the rear some guns were going off, but they seemed a long way off. Forward and away off to the right, beyond some trees, there was some machine-gun fire, and we could see the sharp little orange and blue stabs of flame like electric flashes. It was starting to get light enough so that we could see them dimly.

Meakin waited a moment more before giving the hand signal to move forward.

We stood up slowly all ready to let rip. It was about 50 feet to their position. The machine gun fire had died out as soon as we started to move forward. One of the lads chucked a grenade on the suspected position, which was followed by a pause then boom as flying debris rained back down. We ran forward and there was nothing there. All that build up for absolutely nothing, we gave a quick recce of the area and still found nothing. Everyone had seen the muzzle flashes; the Flip Flops must have bugged out quickly and slipped away without us knowing.

Meakin was a little frustrated that we had come up empty handed, and we knew they were out there somewhere.

I turned to inspect the position and out of the corner on my eye, I spotted something unnatural lying in the ground not 10 feet from where I was standing.

We had no choice but to call the bomb squad. I chatted to one of the guy's I had met way back in training at Catterick, I remember the exact words he said:

"The war of the IED ends up with the loneliest of lonely walks. The last few feet out from your colleagues as you move towards the IED is the loneliest not knowing what to expect.

"Will this IED explode the minute I touch it" type thoughts race through your mind. You are going into a zone that could be your last and any mistake could be your last. The safety equipment you wear will not make the slightest difference to a powerful IED explosion.

At the IED site, you need to focus and put all other thoughts out of your mind to focus on the job at hand.

It often seems like all the Afghan locals seem to know where the IEDs have been planted. They seem to know exactly what parts of a road to avoid when driving along, and ensure they are nowhere near any convoy for fear of getting caught in an IED blast.

In the Afghan heat, the job of diffusing an IED is even harder and there is always the chance of being ambushed. You are never more exposed than when static dealing with an IED."

One funny thing that he told us was that the Pashto word for mine was mine.

The devices the Flip Flops create are nowhere near as complex as those found in Northern Ireland or Iraq. However, they still have the ability to kill and maim.

Normally it is a matter of breaking the link between the pack of batteries wired into the detonator and the container of ammonium nitrate and sugar, or ammonium nitrate and aluminium depending on the recipe used.

Variations abound, the Flip Flops will use both homemade explosive mixtures: pressure plate triggers, release pressure triggers, small devices and much larger ones of 40kg or more explosive.

Some of the defusing methods are almost quaintly old fashioned. No robots to aid diffusion either, the British army thinks more along the lines of cables, hooks and hard work to haul bombs out of the road to a safe distance.

Sometimes the bombs lay hidden for weeks and troops or vehicles pass by unaware they were anything there, and the danger they were in. This one had been placed in a hurry, probably in the hope that as we attacked it would be set off and takes some of us out.

The IED was at least in a position that enabled us to blow it up with some C4. We still had to wait for the bomb disposal team from the Royal Logistics to come and do their bit. That meant possibly a few more hours exposed before we could head back to the safety of the fort.

When it began to get light, the place looked even more discouraging. There was little or no cover, we knew that unless we got some sort of concealment we could be spotted and would become sitting ducks. Most of us started to get hungry and our bellies seemed to rumble in unison. We had only ourselves to blame. We had been told repeatedly never to go anywhere without rations, but we all thought this would be a quick patrol and we'd be home for breakfast.

It was mid-morning before we were finally able to make the trip back to the fort. It seemed for every 10 minutes of action, there was always a fair few hours of nothing. You were always waiting for something or other. Be it a meal a time, going out on patrol or even just waiting for something to happen. Being very patient at times would probably sum it up, although many soldiers would deny this.

There were not many times I was happy to get back to my bed in the now, not quite so smelly cow shed, but this was one of them. I felt completely shattered and my tiredness over ruled my hunger.

I gained another commendation for spotting the IED, and probably saving the lives of many of the lads. All I had done was be observant, and anyone else could have noticed it.

CHAPTER ELEVEN

Practically every soldier carries some kind of mascot or charm. A good many had crucifixes and religious tokens of one type or another. Corporal Fuller had a strange seashell with three little black spots on it. He considered three was his lucky number. Thirteen was mine. My mascot was the much revered cartoon character Garfield. I carried Garfield inside my combat jacket and always felt safer with him there. He hangs at the head of my bed now and I feel better with him there. I realise perfectly that all this sounds like nonsense, and that superstition for many raises an eyebrow.

I figure that if there is anything in war that can help, even a simple mascot, then it is worth doing. I suppose it makes everything that little bit more bearable.

Today we were in for a treat, and a little jolly, the name given for a trip out. Today it was planned that we would move further out than our normal circle of operations. We had been given a couple of new Jackals to go further afield and recee a new area. No reason was given, other than to gather intelligence on any movements close to the border. It was well known that the Flip Flops would often stay just in the border of Pakistan, or use Pakistan as a possible way to get Opium out of the country. The issue was, that the borders were vast and very difficult to police. With the district of Dishu backing onto the Pakistani border there had been intelligence patrols of Flip Flop activity.

As well as gathering intelligence, we were to be a visible presence that may show that British forces were very much in the area. For that reason, this would be a daytime recce patrol.

We had the use of two Jackals, also known as MWMIK (pronounced EmWimmick) or Mobility Weapon-Mounted Installation Kit. The primary role of the vehicle in the British Army was for a rapid assault reconnaissance and fire support roles.

The Jackal is quite an imposing vehicle on first sight and has a distinctive shape. It has no roof to speak of but is very well armoured, even the seats offer some ballistic protection. It was built and designed with Afghanistan in mind and the requirements of that theatre of operation.

The air suspension on the Jackal did a good job of soaking up the rough terrain as we made our way to the recce area.

We all got loaded up and pilled our kit on before making our way towards the Pakistani border. We were out for seven hours and saw nothing, not even a farmer. It is so desolate and baron as soon as you move away from the Helmand River. The river is the reason so many villages have been built along it. The river really is the lifeblood of the province. The picturesque mountains are stunning and even the desert has its own unique, if rugged beauty.

The Jackal driven by Edwards was about to stop short of what was considered a vulnerable area that we needed to Barma. Just as he was about to come to a full stop there was a loud bang and the Jackal just blew up in front of us. There was smoke and dust, and you could see bits of Jackal flying everywhere with three soldiers, including Edwards, flying amongst the debris. We all looked at one another and knew what we were all thinking, "Fuck, no one could survive that." Edwards landed on his head 10 metres away from the explosion - got up and dusted himself off apparently unharmed. Another soldier hit the grenade machine gun as he left the vehicle, shattering his right foot, rupturing his spleen and breaking his pelvis and back. The ballistic plate in his body armour was ripped out and propelled upwards, smashing his teeth and nearly severing his tongue. The final lad landed beside him some 30 metres in front of the Jackal. He had hit the GPMG, which had sliced his left leg off just above the knee. His ballistic plate had broken his right eye socket and he had suffered a broken back.

We all jumped out and Cpl Jones began to Barma towards the casualties, with me carrying a stretcher behind. We needed to get a nine-liner casualty report sent as soon as possible. Edwards was clearly in shock and what he said made no sense whatsoever. All we could do was get everyone patched up and loaded onto our Jackal. I tried to give one of the lad's morphine, but in my own shock, I used the Combo pen the wrong way round and managed to self-administer. We were still trying to get a medical helicopter in and a suitable landing site had been found and Barmed. Finally, an American Black Hawk came in and carried everyone off, less Edwards who said he was fine. However, a few days later Edwards was complaining of persistent headaches, and was taken to Camp Bastion to be examined by a doctor. Edwards was found to have bleeding on the brain, and was sent back to the UK, not returning for the rest of the tour.

We got back to the fort just before dusk; it had been a long and tiring day, "Sightseeing" followed by the horrific sight of Edwards Jackal being blown to pieces. The Mastiff and the Ridgeback were the only vehicles that could truly survive an IED. The Vikings and Jackals were basically widow makers when it came to IEDs.

The next day we had been tasked to help protect a local meeting with various elders from the surrounding area. Two Afghan soldiers in a wooden shack guarded the building. They moved a single strand of razor wire when people were entering or exiting. Waiting inside were elders from the surrounding area. Another reminder of the social complexity of Pashtun tribesmen: each of the representatives was a leader in some capacity, and he wore his tribe's regalia-coloured turbans as tribal identifiers, like Scottish tartans. There was no air conditioning in the building, and the outside temperature was about ninety degrees. They drank piping hot tea and sweated profusely; the room stewing in body odour and the intense musk perfume of the traditional Afghan man. They were there to discuss recent unrest and what support the British Army could give.

There is a cultural oddity in this part of the world that obligates someone to issue the most inoffensive and serene report they can possibly give to a superior, even if it is blatantly or uproariously false. Nobody wanted to admit to trouble. If we had just said hello and closed the meeting after introductions, no one would have complained. Every district representative told us that there were no security problems in their district. The election officials told us that they had surveyed every polling site themselves and that they were all acceptable.

It should have been a great election. It was only after a pointed discussion with Captain Green that the elders and representatives began to confess that yes, some of the villages were not as safe as they could be. The elders still seemed cautious of our support, in essence wanted to solve the problems in Afghanistan without the coalition's help.

It was a sunny, windless day; the nights at the moment were a bit cool. The daytime weather though was very warm. The lads and I were working in the fort, we had recently contracted a local that we knew well to help replace the rotten carpet and paint in the offices, and we were moving every piece of furniture out of our building before we repaired it.

One of the interpreters told the Sergeant that there was a visitor. Our courtyard gate to the fort was open, and he had just wandered in. After being checked for anything that could harm or kill us. His name was Aarmaan and he was from Dishu village. One of the officers came out and said the basic greetings to him in Pashto and shook his hand, the interpreter was a native Pashto speaker. His English wasn't spectacular and at times we struggled to understand what he was saying, although he could communicate with the most isolated and rural villagers.

Aarmaan had come to us because he heard that the British were at the fort and may be able to help. He wanted to speak to one of our officers. It was to do with his father that had recently been shot by some American Special Forces. He explained that four members of his family had also died during the assault. He wanted three things from us. The first was to know if his father was still alive. Then if he was alive, he wanted to know how to get in contact with him or locate him. Finally, he wanted the interpreter to write a letter to the Americans, explaining that he understood that the entire raid had been due to a misunderstanding and wanted to make the American forces aware he only wanted to help and had meant no harm.

Captain Green immediately recognised the situation he was describing. Some SF units had become a bit gun ho and wanted to make their mark, their sometimes gun-ho attitude meant mistakes were being made to the detriment of locals. Usually when SF units identify targets they are supposed to inform the Army unit operating in the area. These units are responsible for patrolling the land - but Afghanistan is such a large country, and there are never enough people to have a presence in every district that we supposedly control. Given that SF has their own dedicated aircraft and support that regular Army units cannot easily access, they are often given the green light on operations. That is often based on intelligence that has only just come in. They can take it out with almost surgical precision, and all we have to do is go and link up with them. We usually police and clear up the mess, and if the target is still alive, the SF takes them for questioning. Sadly, this is not always the case and mistakes do and have occurred.

Aarmaan explained the story to Captain Green, but we were all listening in. He said there were two Flip Flops who fled the scene when they heard the helicopters, and when the SF chased after them and shot them both dead. They were found to be armed with AK-47's and were wearing chest racks of ammunition and grenades. However, they were not part of Aarmaan's family.

The SF then moved toward the house. They ran into the room in which all the men in the compound were sleeping. Supposedly, they had found a hand grenade, but this was after the raid had been completed. Aarmaan was not sure, if someone was holding it, or if the SF just happened to find it. People were yelling and screaming from all angles during the raid. The SF killed four people in one room alone. Aarmaan's father was shot in the same room. He was eighty-seven years old, but was still alive when the SF had finished the attack. The SF realising he was not a threat so took him to the hospital in one of their helicopters.

Captain Green seemed to have developed an affinity with the Afghans. He was from rural Lincolnshire, and after having served and worked with the locals in Iraq, he had come to really appreciate Afghan people. In our welcome brief he referred to them as "rural folk" and said, "How much they cared about their families, all they want is facts and practical solutions." He really believed that understanding them and trying his best to help was the best way to win the war.

Captain Green said, "I can't explain this, what has happened to you is wrong, and I'm sorry. I want the same answers that you do."

Aarmaan like many Afghans was tremendously poor. He could not read or write. He was missing a leg from a Russian mine explosion. His clothes were dirty and he looked dishevelled and unkempt. Captain Green immediately went to the office to make a call. Aarmaan had no last name, and his father's name was Mohammad Qadir. Captain Green was able to locate Aarmaan's father at in a hospital. He came back out and said that he had located Aarmaan's father and that he could go and visit on Mondays and Wednesdays, he just needed to show up at the main entrance to the military hospital at nine in the morning and bring his tazkera, which was a very simple card that formed the national ID system.

Captain Green wrote a letter in English to present to the gate guards. Through the interpreter, Captain Green explained to him how to get to the hospital and what to expect. He also gave Aarmaan some money for the cab fare. Captain Green then asked him if he had any kids. He had six, so Captain Green arranged for some clothes to be brought to the fort for his children if he came back to collect them in two days' time.

He turned round and thanked all of us, Captain Green said he was sorry again, and he left. Aarmaan came back two days later to collect a bundle of children's clothes and you could see by the look in his face how grateful he was. He left with a better impression of the British Army, and another chalk mark for winning the hearts and minds of the locals.

CHAPTER TWELEVE

A general cleaning of rifles started as soon as we sat down for a break. The hot, dry climate and dust could cause stoppages, and regular cleaning was essential. My rifle was in good shape after a quick, clean, and I leaned it against the side of a wall to get to my rations before putting my rifle back together. Whilst I bent down a bullet, ricochet off the wall with a shower of dust and undid all my good work.

I was more annoyed that my clean weapon was now dirty, than the fact, I had probably just cheated death. Everyone thought the bullet had come from a Flip Flop, but actually, Rifleman Jones had forgotten to remove the bullet lodged in the barrel of his rifle and set it off whilst cleaning. This was known as a "Negligent discharge," which was a military offence in itself. Rifleman Jones would most likely get the bollocking of his life followed by a fine.

We were on a pretty normal patrol and as usual the intelligence had said there would be very little if any activity. Flip Flops were still in the area, but our continued patrols, and contact had pushed some of them away, and their presence did seem reduced overall. Then the Flip Flops are slippery creatures and tend to move from one area to the next, undertaking a series of raids and attacks before moving out as reinforcement were brought.

Today we had been given a set area to patrol; intelligence had been gleaned from a local spy of a group of Flip Flops that had taken up a defensive position. Their orders were to take out as many British Army personnel as possible, either by IEDs or shooting us.

Back on patrol, we soon found ourselves on a dusty track outside of Dishu. The track was sunken with banks either side, so provided excellent cover. The sun was shining brilliantly, and it was yet another hot day. The sweat that ran down my face was more like a constant stream than a trickle. You needed to drink constantly to keep rehydrated. We moved up towards the position that the Flip Flops were said to be in, and had been told it may only be two or three at the most. So although on our guard knew we greatly outnumbered them.

As the banks giving us cover, receded and we came out from cover, small arms fire opened up.

Initially it was way off target and we all quickly dropped down on out belt buckles, and fired a few rounds off in the direction of the noise. We then heard the telltale sound of a mortar.

This burst a little behind me, and down went Captain Green and the Sergeant Major with whom he had been talking with. Captain Green died a few days later at Camp Bastion, and the Sergeant Major lost an arm. This was a hard blow right at the start, and it spelt disaster. Everything started to go wrong. Meakin was now in command, and another officer thought that he was in charge. We got conflicting orders, and there was one grand mix-up. Eventually we advanced towards the target. We walked slap-bang into perfectly directed fire. Torrents of machine-gun bullets crackled about us and we went forward with our heads down, like men facing into a storm. Anyone who could come through that had performed a miracle. This was not just two or three Flip Flops, more like ten or twelve determined fighters, and we were in for the firefight of our lives.

Meakin who was close to me, suddenly leaped into the air letting out a hideous yell. He had been struck in the abdomen by a bullet and was dead. I felt terrible about Meakin, as he had been good to all of us. He was the finest type of officer of the British army, the rare sort who can be democratic and yet command respect. He had talked with me often, and I knew about his family and home life. He was more like a big brother to me than a superior officer.

The hail of bullets grew even worse. They whistled, cracked, and squealed, and I began to wonder why on earth I had not been hit? Amazingly, no one else was hit, air support had been called in and we tried to find cover and return fire as best we could.

I have never been so scared in my life. I do not think human beings could find themselves in a more horrific situation than this one. A situation that you have no idea if the next bullet would be the one that ended your life. You could not even see them coming, just hear the whoosh and crack as they flew everywhere. We really were in deep shit.

I was actually praying, to my mascot. I realise that this was plain, unadulterated silly worship, but it shows what a man reverts to in the stress of battle. The total feeling of helplessness and being unable to do anything was the emotions that gripped you the most.

By this time, we were within about 100 feet of the Flip Flops we could see them standing up in a line. Many of us later felt that we had been set up and ambushed. False information had been passed to us, so we fell into a Flip Flop trap.

We were terribly out-manoeuvred - with the loss of the command structure; the pace of our assault had slowed down greatly. One section had decided to see if they could flank the target even though air support was 15 minutes away.

The best thing we could do was cover the flanking section and try our best to stay alive. They had more than just AK47s; there was at least one heavy machine gun. We were lucky that they did not have many mortars or RPGs.

I managed to get myself in a hollow, almost a small hole for better protection. I tried to signal to some of the other lads to join me.

During the few minutes that I lay in that hole, I suffered the worst mental anguish I ever knew. Seeing death and injury and everything go so horribly wrong had nearly broken me. I was dripping with sweat and nauseous. A sudden overpowering impulse seized me to get out in the open, and take on the Flip Flops single handily, just to bring an end to the carnage. I was ready to die.

With air support inbound I should of really stayed where I was. It was a hopeless charge but I had had enough. Fuck to the Flip Flops, I was going in for an attack and did not care less if I was shot or blown to pieces. My fear had been replaced with sheer anger, the red mist had come down and I was going to kill every last one of the Flip Flops.

As I scrambled out of the hole, rounds were impacting all around, some sending splinters off of trees that hit your hands like sharp needles. Then there was a blinding, ear-splitting explosion slightly to my left, and I went down. I did not lose consciousness entirely. A red-hot iron was through my right arm, as if someone had hit me on the left shoulder with a sledgehammer. I felt crushed...shattered.

My impressions of the rest of that day are, for the most part, vague and indistinct; but in spurts, they stand out clear and vivid. The first thing I knew definitely was when Stevens bent over me, cutting the sleeve of my combat jacket.

"It's not too bad, you'll survive," said Stevens. That was some consolation. I was now back in the small hole, and I can remember seeing the silhouette of a Harrier flying over as I gazed into the sky. Followed by a very loud bang, almost in ear splitting distance of where I was. They had not been able to safely pull me far enough back. The explosion was then followed by a ringing in my ears and then an eerie silence that seemed to last a lifetime.

"We'd better get out of here in case any of the Flip Flops survived the bombs," shouted Stevens.

We had walked into a trap and lost two men and two more were injured. Stevens and I got out of the hole and started to crawl. It appeared that he had a wound in his thigh, though he hadn't said anything about it before. We crawled a little way, before feeling safe enough to try to get to our feet. By now, the whole platoon had regrouped and was becoming organised once more. The Sergeant had taken charge and was directing the lads. Some stayed in position providing cover, whilst others moved into the destroyed building to check for survivors. The final group was dedicated to dealing with the casualties. A medevac had been requested and a helicopter was on its way.

The next thing I remember I was on a stretcher. The stretcher swayed and pitched as I was taken away. I passed out and remember my vision just starting to blur before I blacked out. When I came to, my vision was still a bit blurry and I felt light headed and cold even in the heat. I could see the Chinook resting on the grass and soldiers rushing around it. The thump of the two rotors whirring round was unmistakable.

After that, I was put aboard with the others for the ride to Camp Bastion. Snatches of conversation about England and a girl in Wales floated back, then another conversation about going home. I am really not sure if these were conversations I was involved in. So far, I hadn't had much pain, the adrenaline had masked much of the pain I was in. When we landed at Camp Bastion and I was taken to the hospital, the M.O. gave me another going over and said, "You will need to go home to get this one properly sorted. Not sure of any muscle or nerve damage you may have. The wound is very deep and the shrapnel has done a lot of damage."

I had a piece of shrapnel or something through the right upper arm, clearing the bone and making a hole about as big as a one-pound coin. My left shoulder was full of shrapnel fragments, and began to hurt like hell. When I woke up the next time, somebody was sticking a hypodermic needle into my arm.

I spent four days at Camp Bastion awaiting my lift back to the UK. Priority was given to those in greater need of better care and equipment that could be provided in the UK. Whilst I was there, I had a real bath, a genuine hot soapy bath. In addition, I had some shrapnel picked out of my anatomy. I seemed to pick up quite well and wondered why I was being sent home, although I was still in a good deal of dull pain. I was happy to be heading home though, and glad that my war was over.

I shall never forget that wonderful morning when I looked out of the window of the plane and I saw the coast of England, hazy under the mists of dawn. It looked like the Promised Land, and it was. It meant freedom from battle, murder, and sudden death. Freedom from the heat and the smell of that cowshed. I felt sad and guilty to have left behind some good lads, and the losses we had suffered. I had the thoughts and a sense of guilt. Of why I had survived and others had died. Could I have done anything different to prevent their deaths?

As soon as we arrived and got off the plane, I bent down and kissed the tarmac. The feeling to be home was almost overwhelming and brought tears to my eyes.

CHAPTER THIRTEEN

Being back in the UK meant happiness and physical comfort. What I had left behind was death, but I still had to live with the mental images of what I had experienced. From the depths of what seemed like hell I had come home, and I reached my hands with pathetic eagerness to the good things that I had missed. Even going home to Derby seemed appealing.

I never saw a better sight than the faces of those lads, glowing with love, as they strained their eyes for the first sight of UK soil.

A lump swelled in my throat, and I prayed that I might never go back to war. I prayed too that the brave lads still over there might soon be out of it.

It seemed good to look out of the windows and see the signs printed in English. That made it all seem less like a dream.

I was going to Selly Oak hospital. The first thing at the hospital was a real, honest-to-God bath with hot water! Heavens, how I just sat and soaked, the orderly helped me in and had to drag me out. I would have stayed in that bath all night if he would have let me.

The next morning I went around to the M.O. He looked my arm over and calmly said that it might have to come off if gangrene set in. For a moment I wished that piece of shrapnel had gone through my head. I pictured myself going around with only one arm, and the prospect didn't look good.

However, the doctor dressed the arm with the greatest care and I was put on a course of antibiotics.

The nurse in charge of my ward, Nurse Gamble, is one of the finest women I have ever met. I owe it to her care and skill that I still have my good right arm. She made sure my dressings got change regularly and that everything possible was carried out to ensure my wounds healed properly.

My next few weeks were pretty awful. I was in constant pain, and after the old arm began to come around under treatment, one of the doctors discovered that my left hand did not look right. It had been somewhat swollen, but not really bad. The doctor insisted upon an Xray and found a bit of shrapnel imbedded in it. He was all for an operation as the only way to get the shrapnel out and quell the swelling to prevent any further damage.

I was under ether two and a half hours, and when I came out of it the left hand was not good, and hasn't been ever since; some days are better than others. There followed weeks of agonising massage treatments and Physio. Between treatments, though, I had it cushy.

My friends were very good to me, as was everyone at the hospital. Family came to visit me and really helped the rehabilitation of my arm. I cried when I first laid eyes on Helen and the thoughts in Afghanistan that I might never see her again.

Sadly, my time as a soldier was over, my arm and hand would never be able to properly hold a weapon again. Initially, all I wanted to do was to get back to my Battalion, but as time went on, I realised that this was not going to happen. Thankfully, I still had full use of my arm. It may be a little painful at times, but it was still fully usable. I could go back and do some form of desk job, but a medical discharge seemed the most likely.

When I was put on clerical duty, I immediately began to furnish trouble for the British army, not intentionally of course, but quite effective. The first thing I did was to drop a computer and smash it. My hands had times when they absolutely refused to work. They tried me with other forms of clerical duties, which would suit me better, but being an "Office boy" was never my thing and I went back to the MO to ask about a medical discharge.

I had just about given up hope of ever getting out of the army when I was summoned to appear before a Medical Board. You can wager I lost no time in appearing.

The board looked me over with a discouraging and cynical suspicion it seemed. When they gave me a going over, they found that my heart was out of place and that my left hand might never limber up again. They voted for a discharge in no time. In many ways, it felt a bit bittersweet. It was nice to be back on civvy street, but I missed the

Army and the camaraderie that I doubt you find in anything but the armed forces.

It was some weeks before the final formalities were closed up. I then had to wait to find out if any compensation was due

Once free, I lost no time in getting home and making my peace. I was surprised to be welcomed back with open arms. Derby felt like home and I was shocked to find I had actually missed the old city. Even though it felt like I had never been away, I felt 10 years older.

I will never forget the heat and loneliness that I felt in Afghanistan. The frustration, worry, and lack of sleep that I endured day after day. The endless days and nights on patrol or guard, just waiting for the quiet to be shattered by an explosion or gunfire. You almost start wanting it to happen, willing it to happen just to confirm you inner fear. Then when it does happen, you are left empty and drained. You feel like your life force is slowly ebbing away under the constant vigilance that is required each and every day. I have often wondered how much more I can take before I snap and end up in a mental asylum.

When I return home how will I make the transition back to civilian life? What about those around me who are totally unaware of the violence that I have seen and the number I have killed. Will I be a changed person, and what part of me will be left in Afghanistan?

War, by its nature, allows us too much time in between the missions to think. You can end up over thinking and start imagining scenarios that will never occur. The process of being at war strips you of all your emotions. You almost become childlike in terms of your emotions and yearn for your mum when death approaches.

In some ways, I was very lucky. My initiation into war was gradual enough to give me some time to build up mental defences. My fellow soldiers supported my initiation and at times shielded me from the worst the war could throw at us. I know the time to recover mentally will take years, and I suspect and the odd nightmare will probably still happen for the rest of my life.

As a final thought, I have to give a quote that I read in a fallen soldier's diary…

"I know this; I will not allow this experience to affect the rest of my life with bitterness or sorrow. Through the experience I hope I have gained wisdom and will let the experience make me stronger."

Printed in Great Britain
by Amazon

81513362R00051